the Revelation of Jesus Christ

KEITH A. BUTLER

The Revelation of Jesus Christ
Keith A. Butler

ISBN: 978-0-9825028-0-8
EBOOK: 978-0-9825028-1-5

Unless otherwise indicated, all Scripture quotations in
this book are taken from the King James Version (KJV)
of the Holy Bible.

Published by
Word of Faith International Christian Center
20000 W. Nine Mile Road
Southfield, Michigan 48075-5597
www.wordoffaith.cc

Printed in the United States of America

The Revelation of Jesus Christ

KEITH A. BUTLER

word of faith
INT'L CHRISTIAN CENTER

20000 W. Nine Mile Road • Southfield, MI 48075
Pastor André Butler, Senior Pastor
Bishop Keith A. Butler, Founder & Presiding Bishop
Tel.: 248.353.3476 • 24-Hour Prayer: 800.541.PRAY (7729)
To Order: 888.909 WORD (9673)

CONTENTS

Introduction

Many people are frightened by the book of Revelation and will not read it. They think this book is a book of bad news, a book of calamity, and a book of end-time tragedy. Revelation is none of those things. In fact, every Christian is supposed to read, understand, and act on the truths of this book, and those who do so are blessed.

I believe that my children or I–or all of us–will experience what we read about in the book of Revelation. Scripture says that when Jerusalem is no longer trodden down by the Gentiles, then the time of the Gentiles is over. Israel became a nation again on May 14, 1948, with Jews gathering from all four corners of the world where they had been scattered. Jesus says that everything necessary for the true church to be raptured will

1

happen before this generation ceases. There's no strong agreement on how many years a biblical generation is–the number spans from 40 to 120 years and beyond, based on the longevity of some biblical characters. However, regardless of the number, one thing is clear–we are living in the end times.

In a chapter by chapter analysis, I will take you through this book to gain insight into the visions that John sees–from the Lord's instructions to the churches to the New Heaven and the New Earth–in an attempt to motivate you to be ready and to give you an understanding of what is going to occur. We are living in the sliver of time before the rapture of the church. The Lord wants a great awakening, a time when millions of people whose eyes were once closed to God are opened. He wants a great revival to occur that will yield millions of backslidden people back to God. Read, understand and act on these things. God waits to pour out His blessings!

Chapter 1
The Blessing of Revelation

A title to the book of Revelation in my Bible says, *"The Revelation of St. John, The Divine,"* but this is not the revelation of John. Revelation begins with, *"The Revelation of Jesus Christ"* clearly positioning this as divine truth communicated by Jesus Christ. This is truth that God reveals to man.

In the Gospels, Jesus Christ is revealed to us as the Savior. In the epistles, particularly in Paul's epistles, Jesus Christ is revealed as the Head of the Church. Revelation completes the description of His ministry by showing Jesus not only as Head of the Church, but also as the soon coming King of kings and Lord of lords. You cannot have a complete understanding and revelation of the Lord Jesus Christ without this book.

Revelation 1:1
The Revelation of Jesus Christ, which
God gave unto him, to shew unto his
servants things which must shortly come
to pass; and he sent and signified it by
his angel unto his servant John.

Notice that an angel gave this vision to John. Angels are mentioned 188 times in the New Testament, including 55 times in the book of Revelation, making the ministry of angels very prominent in this book and in the events of end-times.

Revelation 1:2-3
Who bare record of the word of God,
and of the testimony of Jesus Christ, and
of all things that he saw. Blessed is he
that readeth, and they that hear the
words of this prophecy, and keep those
things which are written therein: for the
time is at hand.

The Greek word *blessed* means *fortunate and well off*. You need to order your life according to the admonitions and truth in the book of Revelation. You need to make sure you are flowing with God.

The Lord's Instructions

"John to the seven churches which are in Asia" (Revelation 1:4a). The Lord is instructing John to write a letter

to seven churches in Asia Minor. Today, these churches would be located in the country we call Turkey. Each of these churches has certain characteristics representative of all the body of Christ. In other words, there are people in the body of Christ who share characteristics of the seven churches. Of the seven churches, Satan is able to infiltrate six of them. He isn't able to touch one of them, and he will be able to destroy one of them. As you read about these seven churches, see if you have any of their characteristics.

> **Revelation 1:4b**
> Grace be unto you, and peace, from him which is, and which was, and which is to come; and from the seven Spirits which are before his throne.

The seven Spirits that are before the throne of God are symbols of the Holy Spirit. The Holy Spirit is God. Therefore, He is able to be present everywhere. The Holy Ghost is in Heaven and the Holy Ghost is in us now on the Earth. David talked about that very thing in Psalm 139.

> **Psalm 139:7-8**
> Whither shall I go from thy spirit? or whither shall I flee from thy presence? If I ascend up into heaven, thou art there: if I make my bed in hell, behold, thou art there.

In other words, God is God, and the Holy Spirit is the Holy Spirit. God is able to be in more than one place at one time; He is everywhere present. The church is the entity that is hindering the Antichrist. The church is being anointed by, used by and taught by the Holy Spirit.

The Role of the Holy Spirit

In John chapter 16, Jesus talks about the comfort of the Holy Ghost: *"Nevertheless I tell you the truth; It is expedient for you that I go away: for if I go not away, the Comforter will not come unto you; but if I depart, I will send him unto you. And when he is come, he will reprove the world of sin, and of righteousness, and of judgment"* (John 16:7-8).

Without the Holy Spirit, there is no conviction of sin. After the rapture of the church, there will be people who will get saved during that seven-year period. There will be many who will come to know the Lord. The Holy Spirit will be the One that makes sure this is going to happen. He will be on the Earth the entire time.

On the day of Pentecost, all the believers were all filled with the Holy Ghost. They came out of the upper room roaring drunk in the Spirit, laying out on the streets, speaking in tongues in languages of people from many nations.

Acts 2:14-16

But Peter, standing up with the eleven, lifted up his voice, and said unto them, Ye men of Judaea, and all ye that dwell at Jerusalem, be this known unto you, and hearken to my words: For these are not drunken, as ye suppose, seeing it is but the third hour of the day. But this is that which was spoken by the prophet Joel.

What does the prophet Joel say?

Joel 2:28-32

And it shall come to pass afterward, that I will pour out my spirit upon all flesh; and your sons and your daughters shall prophesy, your old men shall dream dreams, your young men shall see visions: And also upon the servants and upon the handmaids in those days will I pour out my spirit.

And I will shew wonders in the heavens and in the earth, blood, and fire, and pillars of smoke. The sun shall be turned into darkness, and the moon into blood, before the great and terrible day of the LORD come.

And it shall come to pass, that whosoever shall call on the name of the LORD shall be delivered: for in mount Zion and

in Jerusalem shall be deliverance, as
the LORD hath said, and in the remnant
whom the LORD shall call.

Here is the beginning of the last days; note that we
have been in these last days for almost 2000 years now.
The Holy Spirit has been doing His work; He has been
getting many saved.

Your Identity in Christ

*"And from Jesus Christ, who is the faithful witness, and
the first begotten of the dead, and the prince of the kings
of the earth. Unto him that loved us, and washed us
from our sins in his own blood" (Revelation 1:5).*

This letter is from the Holy Spirit and from Jesus
Christ Himself, and Jesus Christ is the first begotten
of the dead. If there is a first begotten, then there is a
second and a third begotten and so on.

John 1:14

And the Word was made flesh, and
dwelt among us, (and we beheld his
glory, the glory as of the only begotten
of the Father,) full of grace and truth.

Jesus previously was referred to as the only begotten Son of God, but *John 1:12* says: *"But as many as
received him, to them gave he power* **[authority, right
or privilege]** *to become the sons of God, even to them
that believe on his name."*

There are not separate categories of Sons of God. There is not a class one, class two or class three level. You are either a son of God or you are not a son of God. Jesus was the only begotten Son of God, but because of His death, burial and resurrection, those who will receive Him will also have authority to be sons of God. This means you are no less a son of God than Jesus, the Anointed One. He is your elder brother.

Revelation 1:5a

And from Jesus Christ, who is the faithful witness, and the first begotten of the dead, and the prince of the kings of the earth.

He is King of kings and Lord of lords. He is the Supreme Authority, but there are others that have authority. The kings of the earth are those who have received Jesus as Lord and Savior. Thus, not only has He made those who receive Him sons of the living God, but also kings to rule and operate in authority.

Revelation 1:5b, 6

Unto him that loved us, and washed us from our sins in his own blood, And hath made us kings and priests unto God and his Father; to him be glory and dominion for ever and ever. Amen.

A king's job is to rule. The priest's job is to lead worship and to bring men and women before God Almighty. Not only are you called to be a king, but also you are called to be a priest of the Most High God. Nobody should have to stir you up to worship. Washed from your sins, you ought to worship God all day long!

The Seven Raptures

"Behold he cometh with clouds; and every eye shall see him, and they also which pierced him: and all kindreds of the earth shall wail because of him. Even so, Amen" *(Revelation 1:7).*

Notice Jesus' last message to His disciples on Earth in Acts: *"But ye shall receive power, after that the Holy Ghost is come upon you: and ye shall be witnesses* **[or provide a record]** *unto me both in Jerusalem, and in all Judaea, and in Samaria, and unto the uttermost part of the earth. And when he had spoken these things, while they beheld, he was taken up; and a cloud received him out of their sight. And while they looked stedfastly toward heaven as he went up, behold, two men stood by them in white apparel; Which also said, Ye men of Galilee, why stand ye gazing up into heaven? this same Jesus, which is taken up from you into heaven, shall so come in like manner as ye have seen him go into heaven"* *(Acts 1:8-11).*

This passage tells you a couple of things. One, He is coming back, and two, He will return in the same way He was taken up. The term *rapture* is one I use for *taken up*. The word *rapture* is not in Scripture, but the meaning of the term is clearly there. There are seven raptures in the Scripture:

- Enos was taken up. *(Genesis 5:21-23 and Hebrews 11:5-6)*
- Elijah was taken up. *(2 Kings 2:1,11)*
- The Lord Jesus was taken up. *(Acts 1:9-11)*
- The true church will be taken up at the end of what we call the "church age" before the seven-year period of tribulation called the time of trouble, a term–along with time of testing–used in Revelation. The first three-and-a-half years is called the Tribulation, and the second three-and-a-half years is called the Great Tribulation. *(1 Thessalonians 4:13-18)*
- There will be a mid-tribulation rapture of those who did not go up in the first rapture of the church, but were converted by the preaching of 144,000 converted male, Jewish evangelists. This will produce a worldwide revival where, for every Jew, ten people will grab him and say *"You know something about God. Tell me about Him."* Scripture says that the harvest that is going to take place between the time after the true church is taken up and mid-tribulation will be huge. *(Revelation 7:9-17)*
- The 144,000 Jewish evangelists will be raptured. *(Revelation 14:1-5)*
- Two witnesses will be taken up right before the return of the Lord Jesus Christ to the Earth. *(Revelation 11:1-12)*

The Vision of John

"I am Alpha and Omega, the beginning and the ending, saith the Lord, which is, and which was, and which is to come, the Almighty. I John, who also am your brother, and companion in tribulation, and in the kingdom and patience of Jesus Christ, was in the isle that is called Patmos, for the word of God, and for the testimony of Jesus Christ" (Revelation 1:8-9).

The Apostle John was between the ages of 93 and 97 when the angel came and gave him this prophecy. John was the only one of the disciples that died a natural death, although religious leaders and authorities tried to kill John in numerous ways, including throwing him in a vat of boiling oil. They finally exiled him to the Isle of Patmos, essentially a rock that served as an island for prisoners, with no food, water, or other supplies. They didn't expect him to live long there without any support.

John could have said, *"Woe is me. Lord, I have been faithful to you all these years. I'm cold. I'm hungry and thirsty. I'm living in a cave. What has it profited me to serve you?"* Instead, he begins Revelation chapter one verse 10 saying, *"I was in the Spirit on the Lord's day."* In the New Testament, the Lord's day refers to Sunday. Instead of feeling sorry for himself, this man is praying and in the Holy Ghost. He is having a good time all by himself. He knew how to handle an adverse circumstance.

Revelation 1:10-16

I was in the Spirit on the Lord's day and heard behind me a great voice, as of a trumpet, Saying, I am Alpha and Omega, the first and the last: and, What thou seest, write in a book, and send it unto the seven churches which are in Asia; unto Ephesus, and unto Smyrna, and unto Pergamos, and unto Thyatira, and unto Sardis, and unto Philadelphia, and unto Laodicea.

And I turned to see the voice that spake with me. And being turned, I saw seven golden candlesticks; And in the midst of the seven candlesticks one like unto the Son of man, clothed with a garment down to the foot, and girt about the paps with a golden girdle.

His head and his hairs were white like wool, as white as snow; and his eyes were as a flame of fire. And his feet like unto fine brass, as if they burned in a furnace; and his voice as the sound of many waters. And he had in his right hand seven stars: and out of his mouth went a sharp twoedged sword: and his countenance was as the sun shineth in his strength.

Imagine that you are John and you are doing
your best to describe what you see. He sees a number
of things: seven golden candlesticks, that refer to the
churches. He also sees seven stars that refer to the angels. The purpose of the candlestick is to give light, and
that is the purpose of the church. If the church doesn't
bring light to its community, light to ignorance and
darkness, and if it doesn't reveal God, His Word and His
plan, it is of no value.

Notice also, and this is going to be important later,
that out of Jesus' mouth–the image John is describing–
is a sharp, two-edged sword. A double-edged sword cuts
both ways. My teaching style follows that of Jesus: I will
teach you not only what the Word is telling you, but also
I will give you the reverse meaning. Thus, if the Word
says that you are blessed if you do something, I will tell
you that there's a curse if you don't do that.

Revelation 1:17-20

And when I saw him, I fell at his feet as
dead. And he laid his right hand upon
me, saying unto me, Fear not; I am the
first and the last: I am he that liveth, and
was dead; and, behold, I am alive for
evermore, Amen; and have the keys of
hell and of death.

Write the things which thou hast seen,
and the things which are, and the things
which shall be hereafter; The mystery of

the seven stars which thou sawest in my
right hand, and the seven golden candlesticks. The seven stars are the angels
of the seven churches: and the seven
candlesticks which thou sawest are the
seven churches.

Some people think that when they read about the
angel of the church that it is referring to the pastor, but
it is not. The Greek word here, *angelos*, means *angel*.
The angels provide assistance to the pastor and to the
church. The angels provide help to all individuals who
are born-again, as we see in *Hebrews chapter one, verses
13-14: "But to which of the angels said he at any time,
Sit on my right hand, until I make thine enemies thy
footstool? Are they not all ministering spirits, sent forth
to minister for them who shall be heirs of salvation?"*

If you are an heir of salvation, God has assigned
you an angel that has been involved in your life to the
degree that you have allowed him to work for you. You
have something to say about what he does or doesn't get
to do. Scripture tells you that you will eventually judge
your angel. But I wouldn't be too fast to get on his case,
lest he bring out the cameras, roll back the tape and
document what you've been saying and doing!

Chapter 2 • Revelation 2
The Seven Churches 1.0

J esus sets the following pattern by which He will speak to each one of these churches: **(1)** He commends them for their characteristics that please Him. **(2)** He calls attention to what displeases Him. **(3)** He calls for them to repent. **(4)** He warns them about the price of disobedience if they don't. Notice also that this is also a pattern by which God deals with you. It is important that you think rightly about who God is and what He desires for you.

When I was a boy, I thought God was just a mean judge sitting on the throne waiting for me to do something wrong so He could punish me. That is the image I had because all I heard was, *"God is going to get you."* I thought God would put a person in a test or trial that would leave them half dead because He wanted to teach him something. The adults would teach me that about God, then say, *"Now love that creature."* Instinctively, I knew there was something that wasn't quite lining up, but I was young and didn't know what to do about it. I didn't have any light or revelation, and there wasn't any clear teaching from God's Word.

Let's look at each of these churches in depth and see what we can learn about pleasing God.

The Church at Ephesus

Jesus is walking throughout the first church. Let's look at its characteristics: *"Unto the angel of the church of Ephesus write; These things saith he that holdeth the seven stars in his right hand, who walketh in the midst of the seven golden candlesticks. I know thy works, and thy labour, and thy patience, and how thou canst not bear them which are evil: and thou hast tried them which say they are apostles, and are not, and hast found them liars" (Revelation 2:1-2)*

Losing Your First Love

Look what God says in verse 3: *"And hast borne, and hast patience, and for my name's sake hast laboured, and hast not fainted. Nevertheless I have somewhat against thee, because thou hast left thy first love" (Revelation 2:3-4).*

Jesus was asked, *"Master, what is the greatest commandment in the Torah?"*

Matthew 22:37, 39
Jesus said unto him, Thou shalt love the
Lord thy God with all thy heart, and with
all thy soul, and with all thy mind . . . And
the second is like unto it, Thou shalt love
thy neighbour as thyself.

The second commandment is just as important as the first; in fact, the second commandment comes about because loving God with all your heart means that what is important to God is important to you. To lose your first love means that God and His agenda are no longer the number one priority in your life. This church at Ephesus had lost its zeal for God and zeal for God's program.

1 Timothy 2:3-4
For this is good **[beautiful]** and acceptable in the sight of God our Saviour;
Who will have all men to be saved, and
to come unto the knowledge of the
truth.

Notice two things about the will of God. *First*, it is His will that all men be delivered, healed, preserved, made sound and made whole. *Second*, He wants all to come into complete and total knowledge of the truth. The love of God's heart is to get people saved and to have their eyes opened, so they can see the real truth in a world full of error and darkness.

So a church that is in love with the Lord is a church that is involved in witnessing every chance it can get, because how can people be saved without a preacher. A preacher doesn't refer just to a prophet, evangelist, pastor or teacher. Every born-again person is a preacher, because a *preacher* is a *proclaimer*. Your job is to proclaim the Lord and to educate and disciple people in the truth so that they can turn around and share the Gospel with others.

If you are in a church that doesn't do those two things or at least teach people to do those two things—if you are in a church that has a lot of religious activity, but is an Ephesus church—you need to find another church.

This wasn't a church that prayed, either. They had a lot of religious activity but didn't do the things that really constituted Jesus' church: *witness, teach, and pray.* Again, this church did have some good things happening. They had patience and some works, but their hearts were not really in it.

Remembering Life Without God

"Nevertheless I have somewhat against thee, because thou hast left thy first love. Remember therefore from whence thou art fallen and repent, and do the first works." (Revelation 2:4-5a).

In other words, *"Go back and remember who you were, what life was like before you received the light and life of God. Don't forget how wretched and messed up you were before you got saved.*

If you were like I was when I first got saved, you started telling everybody what God had done. The week after I got saved, I was out in the street with my buddies and one of them said, *"Let's go do this."*

I said, *"No I can't do that."*

The next week, one of them said, *"Let's go do this."* I said, *"No I can't do that, either."*

After repeated invitations, they finally said, *"What is up with you?"*

I said, *"I got saved."*

"Oh no. No. You got saved? You got saved?"

"Yea, I got saved."

"You won't last two weeks," they said.

I've been following God almost forty years now. I guess they were wrong!

Notice what Jesus said next: *"Or else I will come unto thee quickly, and will remove thy candlestick out of his place, except thou repent" (Revelation 2:5b).*

Jesus not only establishes the church, but also removes churches when they lose their value to the kingdom. If a church doesn't witness, doesn't cause people to learn the truth, doesn't pray, and if a church is only formed by customs and catering to the flesh, not advancing the kingdom of God, the Lord doesn't want His name on it.

You can look at the histories of some churches and some denominations and see that they started out on fire for God, doing the great works of God. Today those denominations are totally cold and losing members. What happened? Their candlesticks were removed.

The only way that you can do the works of God is
if the Lord builds the church. If the Lord doesn't build
the church, you are in vain to build it. You can build
a church in the flesh, but there will be no credit, no
anointing, no move of God and no revelation. It will be
only an institution.

If the Lord removes a church, He will send someone
else to be His witness, because He still wants all men to
be saved and come to the knowledge of the truth. That
is the reason why you will see three or four churches in
the same place.

Hating Evil Deeds

*"But this thou hast, that thou hatest the deeds of the
Nicolaitans, which I also hate" (Revelation 2:6).*

If God hates something, then you are supposed to
hate it. The Nicolaitans were known for their lascivious
lifestyle, for false teaching and for error. They wanted
the priesthood to be restored, but they wanted the
church to be controlled by laymen. Nicholas, the deacon,
was their leader.

Men elected by men are not supposed to rule men
called by God. When you have laypersons trying to run
what God planted, you will never get what God wanted
to happen, because they aren't called and anointed for
that role.

Just because someone is a successful business-
man doesn't mean that person knows anything about
the anointing of God and the plan that God has for the
church.

God hates religion. Christianity is not a religion. Religion is comprised of forms, customs and religious activity. Christianity is an experience with Someone that is alive, Someone who will change your life forever. His name is Jesus Christ. In Luke, you see the attitude that causes religion.

> **Luke 10:38-40a**
> Now it came to pass, as they went, that he entered into a certain village: and a certain woman named Martha received him into her house. And she had a sister called Mary, which also sat at Jesus' feet, and heard his word. But Martha was cumbered about much serving.

Jesus and His disciples, and maybe even more of His travelling companions, are all in the house and Martha is running around asking, *"Do you have enough drinks? Can I get you anything to eat?"* While she is doing all this, she comes to Jesus and says, *"Lord, dost thou not care that my sister hath left me to serve alone"* *(Luke 10:40b)?*

Religion has a controlling spirit. It has wrong priorities. Did Jesus say, *"Now, Mary, you can't let Martha do all the work by herself. Get up and go help her."* No, He said, *"Martha, Martha, thou art careful and troubled about many things: But one thing is needful: and Mary hath chosen that good part, which shall not be taken away from her" (Luke 10:41-42).*

Mary may not have had everything in order, but there was one thing she did get right. She loved God, and she wanted to have His Words so that she could do His works. That is the difference between religion and true worship. We have a program at our churches, but at any time and in any situation, we can stop what we're doing and follow what God's Spirit is saying to do. Service doesn't have to end in 90 minutes, and it doesn't have to end in 240 minutes. It needs to end only when the Holy Ghost wants it to be over.

> **Revelation 2:7**
> He that hath an ear, let him hear what the Spirit saith unto the churches; To him that overcometh to him will I give to eat of the tree of life, which is in the midst of the paradise of God.

The word *overcometh* means *one that prevails, one that gets the victory.* This person may be in the middle of all kind of things that are not pleasing to the Lord, but this particular individual prevails.

We last saw the phrase *"tree of life"* in Genesis chapter three when God banished Adam and Eve from the Garden lest they ate from the tree of life and live forever. The overcomer has eternal life; he gets to eat of the tree of life.

The Church at Smyrna
"And unto the angel of the church in Smyrna write;

These things saith the first and the last, which was dead, and is alive; I know thy works, and tribulation, and poverty, (but thou art rich) and I know the blasphemy of them which say they are Jews, and are not, but are the synagogue of Satan" (Revelation 2:8-9).

Smyrna is the persecuted church. There are churches today, or portions of the body of Christ today, that are undergoing serious, physical persecution. I have preached in some of these nations where a person can lose a job, family, home and life for being a Christian. There are those within this church who are of the synagogue of Satan.

Being Faithful Unto Death

"Fear none of those things which thou shalt suffer: behold, the devil shall cast some of you into prison, that ye may be tried; and ye shall have tribulation ten days: be thou faithful unto death, and I will give thee a crown of life" (Revelation 2:10). When God says to be faithful unto death, He's just told you how long He expects you to stay there. In other words, He's saying, *"I expect you to stick with Me even in the middle of this trouble until you die."*

Revelation 2:11
He that hath an ear, let him hear what the Spirit saith unto the churches; He that overcometh shall not be hurt of the second death.

25

He that overcomes, he that prevails over the tribulation, will escape the second death.

Revelation 20:11-12
And I saw a great white throne, and him that sat on it, from whose face the earth and the heaven fled away; and there was found no place for them.

And I saw the dead, small and great, stand before God; and the books were opened: and another book was opened, which is the book of life: and the dead were judged out of those things which were written in the books, according to their works.

This is the *Great White Throne* judgment for those who are not overcomers; it is for those who have not made the decision to receive and stick with Jesus Christ. He said the books—plural—will be opened. There is a record of everything you have done in your life: every thought, action, intent and word is recorded, and it will be judged against the Bible. The Bible will judge your hearts, your actions, your motives and your words.

Calling every molecule back together and fitting it all in a human body is no problem to God: *"And the sea gave up the dead which were in it; and death and hell delivered up the dead which were in them: and they were judged every man according to their works" (Revela-*

tion 20:13). There will be, and there are now, people in hell who will stand before this judgment in Revelation chapter 20 and be given a full picture of why they are in Hell.

There are some popular teachings across the country that say there is no placed called Hell, that a loving God would never send any person to Hell. ***God is love.*** Hell was not created for man originally; it was created for Satan and his angels. Anybody who **decides** to follow him and not God will join Satan in Hell. **If you turn away from the living God and get Satan's judgment, you have chosen Hell for yourself.** Make a decision for the Lord and reject Satan. Hell is a real place, but it is not the end.

Revelation 20:14-15

And death and hell were cast into the lake of fire. This is the second death. And whosoever was not found written in the book of life was cast into the lake of fire.

No matter what your situation, even if you are facing horrible persecution, stick with God all the way. Know that believers are praying for you every day, that God will provide a supernatural exit and supernatural provision for you. Do not fear, but don't stand and say, *"I don't belong to Jesus."* If necessary, you must even be willing to give up your life. There is no way Satan or his Antichrist is going to win.

The Church at Pergamos

"And to the angel of the church in Pergamos write; These things saith he which hath the sharp sword with two edges; I know thy works, and where thou dwellest, even where Satan's seat is: and thou holdest fast my name, and hast not denied my faith, even in those days wherein Antipas was my faithful martyr, who was slain among you, where Satan dwelleth. But I have a few things against thee, because thou hast there them that hold the doctrine of Balaam, who taught Balac to cast a stumblingblock before the children of Israel, to eat things sacrificed unto idols, and to commit fornication" (Revelation 2:12-14).

The main problem with the church of Pergamos is that it is involved in idol worship. Remember, the first of the Ten Commandments is, *"Thou shall have no other god before me."* Pergamos is a place of strong Satanic activity. Many times when people see the word *fornication* they think only in terms of sex, but the word Greek word *porneia* means *to act as a harlot or to indulge in unlawful lust, either sexually or in idolatry.* In biblical times, people worshiped almost everything: suns, moons, animals, and so forth, which was a practice they had adopted from the cultures around them. They were eating in honor of these idols. They were associating with idolaters in the heathen temple. In other words, they were going places they weren't supposed to be. They partook with them in their religious festivals, following teachings that led them into idolatry and lasciviousness.

Revelation 2:15-17
So hast thou also them that hold the doctrine of the Nicolaitans. Repent; or else I will come unto thee quickly, and will fight against them with the sword of my mouth.

He that hath an ear, let him hear what the Spirit saith unto the churches; To him that overcometh will I give to eat of the hidden manna, and will give him a white stone, and in the stone a new name written, which no man knoweth saving he that receiveth it.

Manna refers to *supernatural provisions.* Supernatural provision and authority are given to overcomers.

The Church at Thyatira
"And unto the angel of the church in Thyatira write; These things saith the Son of God, who hath his eyes like unto a flame of fire, and his feet are like fine brass; I know thy works, and charity, and service, and faith, and thy patience, and thy works; and the last to be more than the first. Notwithstanding I have a few things against thee, because thou sufferest that woman Jezebel, which calleth herself a prophetess, to teach and to seduce my servants to commit fornication, and to eat things sacrificed unto idols" (Revelation 2:18-20).

Thyatira is a corrupt, self-promoting church, and Jezebel is a self-promoter who calls herself a prophetess. The Holy Ghost is the promoter. If you are always trying to promote yourself, to get to the pulpit or to do something so that you are noticed, you will not get very far. The Holy Ghost gives you the gifts. He gives you the talents you have. He gives you favor where favor is necessary. Your responsibility is to do what your hands can find to do, and do it with all your might.

Once again, the real problem is idolatry, with people teaching doctrines contrary to the Lordship of Jesus. But what I find particularly instructive is what the Lord says: *"And I gave her space to repent of her fornication; and she repented not" (Revelation 2:21).*

In other words, God gave her time. The book of Romans says it this way: *"The goodness of God leadeth thee to repentance" (Romans 2:4b).* Just because the hammer doesn't fall when you are doing what you shouldn't be doing doesn't mean that you are getting away with anything. God may be giving you time and space to come to your senses and understand what you are doing.

Revelation 2:22
Behold, I will cast her into a bed, and them that commit adultery with her into great tribulation, except they repent of their deeds.

Jezebel is the center of the problem, but there were folks that decided to follow along with her idolatry.

Again, Scripture talks about idolatry in the form of fornication and adultery. You are married to God. If you have any other before Him, you have entered into fornication and adultery. Nothing–no one, no situation, no thing–is supposed to come before God.

The tribulation period begins immediately upon the rapture of the church. When you read these letters to the churches, remember that He is talking to born-again people. Some people in the body of Christ assume that just because you were saved at some point, you automatically go up in the rapture of the church, regardless of what you do after you were saved. That isn't true at all.

> **Revelation 2:23**
> And I will kill her children with death; and all the churches shall know that I am he which searcheth the reins **[the mind and thoughts]** and hearts **[motives]**: and I will give unto every one of you according to your works.

Again, Jezebel is a self-promoter, and everything she does is from the wrong motive. It matters not only what you do, but why you do it. You can do things to be seen. You can do things to get yourself in line for something you want. Jezebel's motives are absolutely wrong, and those who have her spirit are wrong.

You have to watch who you hang around with, because you will soon start becoming what they

are. If you hang around a Jezebel spirit, you will become Jezebel.

Revelation 2:24-29

But unto you I say, and unto the rest in Thyatira, as many as have not this doctrine, and which have not known the depths of Satan, as they speak; I will put upon you none other burden. But that which ye have already hold fast till I come.

And he that overcometh, and keepeth my works unto the end, to him will I give power over the nations: And he shall rule them with a rod of iron; as the vessels of a potter shall they be broken to shivers: even as I received of my Father. And I will give him the morning star. He that hath an ear, let him hear what the Spirit saith unto the churches.

Notice several things here. This individual will have authority over the nations, and he will rule them with a rod of iron. The individuals who overcome will rule and reign with Christ. Not every believer during the Millennium, the thousand-year rule of Christ, will be in leadership. There are descriptions of Christians in Revelation, and some have crowns and some don't. Some have only white robes. Why? There are different categories of Christians, and as a man does, that is what he is going to reap.

Chapter 3 • Revelation 3
The Seven Churches 2.0

I n the last chapter, we looked at four of the seven churches in Revelation chapter two. The church at Ephesus had forsaken its first love; the church at Smyrna was the persecuted church; the church at Pergamos needed to repent; and the church at Thyatira tolerated the woman Jezebel, the false prophetess and self-promoter. Note that all of these churches allowed the problems to continue. They didn't deal with what was going on in the congregation. In this chapter, we're going to look at the final three churches.

The Church of Sardis
"And unto the angel of the church in Sardis write; These things saith he that hath the seven Spirits of God, and

the seven stars" (Revelation 3:1a). There is only one Spirit, but there are many different manifestations of the Spirit, as we see in *1 Corinthians 12:4-7: "Now there are diversities of gifts, but the same Spirit. And there are differences of administrations, but the same Lord. And there are diversities of operations, but it is the same God which worketh all in all. But the manifestation of the Spirit is given to every man to profit withal."*

These are the expressions of the Spirit. There are gifts and ministries. There are operations of the Spirit. The book of Isaiah says that a number of these expressions are upon the Lord Jesus. And indeed, John tells you that the Holy Spirit is called a *Comforter [Counselor, Helper, Intercessor, Advocate, Strengthener, and Standby] (John 14:16, The Amplified Bible).*

Isaiah 11:1 talks about the Spirit that was on Jesus. *Acts 10:38* tells us how God anointed Jesus of Nazareth with the Holy Ghost. *Jesus had the Spirit of Wisdom, the Spirit of Understanding, the Spirit of Counsel, the Spirit of Might, the Spirit of Knowledge, and the Spirit of the Fear of the Lord.* In other words, the seven Spirits it refers to in *Revelation 3:1* are the Holy Spirit and His numerous manifestations; He is God.

Revelation 3:1b
I know thy works, that thou hast a name
that thou livest, and art dead.

The church of Sardis is the dead church. They say they are alive, but they are dead. They have an outward form and a profession, but that is all they have. There is no power. There is nothing real about it whatsoever. Now again, we are talking about the church that has moved from what God wanted it be and has become just a church of forms, customs, show and religion.

Revelation 3:2-3
Be watchful, and strengthen the things which remain, that are ready to die: for I have not found thy works perfect before God. Remember therefore how thou hast received and heard, and hold fast, and repent. If therefore thou shalt not watch, I will come on thee as a thief, and thou shalt not know what hour I will come upon thee.

Nobody knows the exact time or day of the coming of the Lord. But note that here He says that they wouldn't even know what season or hour it was. In other words, this church has moved so far away from any revelation or understanding of the Spirit that they don't even know it is the last days and that the return of the Lord is nigh. They are just moving through their days, totally blind to all spiritual truth and understanding.

Revelation 3:4-5a
Thou hast a few names even in Sardis which have not defiled their garments; and they shall walk with me in white: for

they are worthy. He that overcometh,
the same shall be clothed in white raiment; and I will not blot out his name
out of the book of life.

The Bible is the Book of Life. Your name is in this book. If He has to say *"I will not blot out your name out of the Book of Life,"* that must mean that your name can be blotted out, that you can lose your salvation. Once again, just because you were once saved doesn't mean you'll go up in the rapture. He is telling this church that their lethargy and religion could cause them to become totally backslidden and return to the ways of the world.

This is not easy to do, especially with the mercy, long-suffering and grace of the Lord, but it is possible. You don't want to be the dead church.

Revelation 3:5
He that overcometh, the same shall be
clothed in white raiment; and I will not
blot out his name out of the book of life,
but I will confess his name before my
Father, and before his angels.

The word *confess* means *to acknowledge* before His Father and before His angels. Look at what happens when your God acknowledges you: *"He that hath my commandments, and keepeth them, he it is that loveth me: and he that loveth me shall be loved of my Father, and I will love him, and will manifest myself to him"*

(John 14:21). When you have the Father manifesting or appearing on your behalf, your point of need is not going to be there very long! The power of God will show up and show out. God will acknowledge that power in front of men. We see that in *Psalm 23* where the Psalmist says, *"I will prepare a table before you in the presence of your enemies."* In other words, *"I am going to show everybody that you belong to me by what I do. The table is set in front of you and in front of your enemies."* God wants to manifest Himself to you and through you.

The Church of Philadelphia
"He that hath an ear, let him hear what the Spirit saith unto the churches. And to the angel of the church in Philadelphia write; These things saith he that is holy, he that is true, he that hath the key of David, he that openeth, and no man shutteth; and shutteth, and no man openeth" (Revelation 3:6-7). He that is holy and true; he that has the key of David and opens and shuts–this is no one other than Jesus.

Revelation 3:8-9
I know thy works: behold, I have set before thee an open door, and no man can shut it: for thou hast a little strength, and hast kept my word, and hast not denied my name. Behold, I will make them of the synagogue of Satan, which say they are Jews, and are not, but do lie; behold, I will make them to come

and worship before thy feet, and to
know that I have loved thee.

In other words, this church is going to have manifestations of God. Man cannot stop what God is going to
do.

Those going the wrong way, those going the false
way, are going to come, see and know that God's hand
is on you. God said, *"I am going to put them right at
your feet."* This is an overcoming church. This is a Word
church, a faithful church and a true church.

Faithfulness is the *character quality that ensures
that you do the right thing*, whether anyone is watching
you or not, whether anyone is keeping tabs or not. When
you are faithful, you do things with the right motive,
and you can be counted on all the time.

Everybody in the body of Christ likes people who
are faithful, especially pastors. I know that I can give
the faithful something to do and don't have to think
about it any more!

Revelation 3:10-11
Because thou hast kept the word of my
patience, I also will keep thee from the
hour of temptation, which shall come
upon all the world, to try them that dwell
upon the earth. Behold, I come quickly:
hold that fast which thou hast, that no
man take thy crown.

Again, the power of temptation or the hour of testing refers to the tribulation. Those who remain faithful will have a crown.

> **Revelation 3:12**
> Him that overcometh will I make a pillar in the temple of my God, and he shall go no more out: and I will write upon him the name of my God, and the name of the city of my God, which is new Jerusalem, which cometh down out of heaven from my God: and I will write upon him my new name.

Jesus comes again two times—at the beginning of the tribulation, and on the last day when He appears at Armageddon to do some battle. When it is battle time, He is going to have His name, His new authority, written on His thigh. This church will have all the authority that He has.

You want to have the characteristics of this church at Philadelphia. This is a Word church. It is a love church.

The Church of Laodicea

"And unto the angel of the church of the Laodiceans write; These things saith the faithful and true witness, the beginning of the creation of God; I know thy works, that thou art neither cold nor hot: I would thou wert cold or hot. So then because thou art lukewarm, and neither

cold nor hot, I will spue thee out of my mouth" (Revelation 3:14-16).

The word *spue* means *to vomit you up.* In order to vomit something, you had to have ingested it at some point. It was in you. It was part of you, but it became so troubling to you that it had to come out.

Why does He say that He wishes this church were either hot or cold? If you were one or the other, He could do something about it.

Revelation 3:17a
Because thou sayest, I am rich, and increased with goods, and have need of nothing.

This church is prosperous and has allowed its prosperity to dull it. I have been in the ministry my whole adult life, and I have seen this time and time again. Many times people start out working hard and experience success. They experience blessings. The pressure isn't on them any more. Their bills are paid, and things are going well. That zeal becomes dulled, and they become lukewarm. To God, being lukewarm means that you were on fire and then you became cold because good things were happening. You became prosperous. You were enjoying good health. Your children were doing well. Life was good. And instead of that firing you up, you became lukewarm.

God is not against prosperity, but He is against prosperity changing you. I had a man in my church one time who didn't have anything going for him. He wanted to learn the Word of God, so I taught him. He became prosperous; in fact, he became a millionaire. But when He became wealthy, his zeal disappeared. I stopped seeing him at church because he had other things to do. The end result was that he became very cold to the things of God and backslid. He ended his life by committing suicide. Yes, it is possible to go from being hot to being dead.

Revelation 3:17b-19a

And knowest not that thou art wretched, and miserable, and poor, and blind, and naked: I counsel thee to buy of me gold tried in the fire, that thou mayest be rich; and white raiment, that thou mayest be clothed, and that the shame of thy nakedness do not appear; and anoint thine eyes with eyesalve, that thou mayest see. As many as I love, I rebuke and chasten.

The Lord said, *"If I love you, I will rebuke you."* People transpose this statement. They think that love means allowing people to do what they want and never saying a cross word, but God doesn't love that way. The Lord will chasten you, and He chastens you with His Word. Let's take a look at Hebrews chapter 12.

Hebrews 12:1-2
Wherefore seeing we also are compassed about with so great a cloud of witnesses, let us lay aside every weight, and the sin which doth so easily beset us, and let us run with patience the race that is set before us,

Looking unto Jesus the author and finisher of our faith; who for the joy that was set before him endured the cross, despising the shame, and is set down at the right hand of the throne of God.

Instead of asking God to take away the weight, you are to lay it aside. In other words, you are to make up your mind and act. Jesus had the strength to endure the beatings and the crucifixion by focusing on what God was going to give Him. You get through tough times in the same manner as Jesus. You have to look at the joy. You have to see your future reward. You can't look at what is in front of you, but look at what is coming for you.

Hebrews 12:3-4
For consider him that endured such contradiction of sinners against himself, lest ye be wearied and faint in your minds. Ye have not yet resisted unto blood, striving against sin.

Jesus resisted in that Garden of Gethsemane until His sweat was almost as big as great drops of blood. It's possible that his pores opened, and he actually sweated blood. The pressure on Him to avoid crucifixion was immense, but He resisted it.

Hebrews 12:5-8
And ye have forgotten the exhortation which speaketh unto you as unto children, My son, despise not thou the chastening of the Lord, nor faint when thou art rebuked of him: For whom the Lord loveth he chasteneth, and scourgeth every son whom he receiveth.

If ye endure chastening, God dealeth with you as with sons; for what son is he whom the father chasteneth not? But if ye be without chastisement [education and training] whereof all are partakers, then are ye bastards, and not sons.

A *bastard* is an *illegitimate child.* God said, *"You aren't mine if you don't receive chastening, or the 'exhortation which speaketh.'"* God does not chasten with sickness and disease, poverty and lack or fear and depression. He uses the Word.

Hebrews 12:9
Furthermore we have had fathers of our

flesh which corrected us, and we gave
them reverence: shall we not much
rather be in subjection unto the Father
of spirits, and live?

You are a spirit, and the chastisement goes to your
spirit. I have been chastened by God, and I would rather
have been the recipient of a belting than to hurt so in
my spirit being when He set me straight with the Word.

Revelation 3:19
As many as I love, I rebuke and chasten:
be zealous therefore, and repent.

The next verse is a verse that I have heard
preached as an altar call for the sinner, but when you
see the context, you realize it has nothing to do with the
sinner, even though millions have been saved with this
invitation: *"Behold, I stand at the door, and knock: if
any man hear my voice, and open the door, I will come in
to him, and will sup with him, and he with me"* (Revelation 3:20).

The Lord is standing outside the lukewarm Laodicea church saying, *"You have kicked me out. If you let
me back in, we will have dinner together and I will share
with you my revelation."*

Revelation 3:21
To him that overcometh will I grant to
sit with me in my throne, even as I also

overcame, and am set down with my
Father in his throne.

Jesus is seated at the throne, the right hand of God, which is the seat of all authority and power in the universe. The overcomer is on a throne next to Jesus. The overcomer, the true church, has a throne and authority just like the Father. They rule; they reign.

Reader, do everything you need to do in order to be an overcomer. Be true to God. Stay in His Word. Be guided by the Holy Spirit. Stay faithful unto the end.

Chapter 4 • Revelation 4
The Rapture of the True Church

In this chapter, we're going to look at several New Testament passages that speak to the rapture of the true church before we look at the scene in Revelation chapter four. The Holy Spirit, through the writers of the New Testament, has been encouraging, exhorting and preparing His people for this event: *"Behold, I shew you a mystery; We shall not all sleep, but we shall all be changed, In a moment, in the twinkling of an eye, at the last trump: for the trumpet shall sound, and the dead shall be raised incorruptible, and we shall be changed. (1 Corinthians 15:51-52).*

This change happens at light speed—in the *twinkling* of an eye. The blinking of an eye is too slow. Physicists know that there is something beyond the speed of light, which is 186,000 miles per second. It is called eternity. There is no time with God because everything moves so fast. This transformation will happen so suddenly that you won't have time to say, *"I repent."* By the time you open your mouth, the raptured will be gone. **You want to live in a state of readiness.**

1 Corinthians 15:53-58
For this corruptible shall put on incorruption, and this mortal must put on immortality. So when this corruptible shall have put on incorruption, and this mortal shall have put on immortality, then shall be brought to pass the saying that is written, Death is swallowed up in victory.

O death, where is thy sting? O grave, where is thy victory? The sting of death is sin; and the strength of sin is the law. But thanks be to God, which giveth us the victory through our Lord Jesus Christ.

Therefore, my beloved brethren, be ye stedfast, unmoveable, always abounding in the work of the Lord, forasmuch as ye know that your labour is not in vain in the Lord.

Right now our bodies are corruptible; they decay. After the rapture, our mortal bodies shall put on immortality. We will go from having a decaying body to having one like Jesus. Because Jesus is an overcomer, you can be victorious, too!

Stay Untroubled

"Let not your heart be troubled: ye believe in God, believe also in me. In my Father's house are many mansions: if it were not so, I would have told you. I go to prepare a place for you. And if I go and prepare a place for you, I will come again, and receive you unto myself; that where I am, there ye may be also" (John 14:1-3).

Note these things. He said, *"I am going to prepare,"* and then He said, *"I will come again. I will receive you unto me so you can be where I am."* You can clearly see that there is a catching away; there is a taking up. Let's look at First Thessalonians, chapter four:

1 Thessalonians 4:13-18
But I would not have you to be ignorant, brethren, concerning them which are asleep, that ye sorrow not, even as others which have no hope. For if we believe that Jesus died and rose again, even so them also which sleep in Jesus will God bring with him.

For this we say unto you by the word of the Lord, that we which are alive and remain unto the coming of the Lord shall not prevent them which are asleep.

> For the Lord himself shall descend from
> heaven with a shout, with the voice of
> the archangel, and with the trump of
> God: and the dead in Christ shall rise
> first: Then we which are alive and re-
> main shall be caught up together with
> them in the clouds, to meet the Lord in
> the air: and so shall we ever be with the
> Lord. Wherefore comfort one another
> with these words.

The words *comfort one another* mean *to exhort one another*. Notice several things: *first*, the capturing, or the rapture, or the taking up of the church in the resurrection of all of the righteous since Adam occurs at the same time. Thus, all of the saints, including those who are alive at this time, shall be caught up in the clouds to meet the Lord in the air. They are going to be with Him as He is.

Be Ready

In *Matthew 24:36,* the Lord Jesus is speaking. Notice what He says: *"But of that day and hour knoweth no man, no, not the angels of heaven, but my Father only."* God has a time that has not yet been revealed to us.

Matthew 24:44-51

> Therefore be ye also ready: for in such
> an hour as ye think not the Son of man
> cometh. Who then is a faithful and wise

servant, whom his lord hath made ruler over his household, to give them meat in due season? Blessed is that servant, whom his lord when he cometh shall find so doing. Verily I say unto you, That he shall make him ruler over all his goods.

But and if that evil servant shall say in his heart, My lord delayeth his coming; And shall begin to smite his fellowservants, and to eat and drink with the drunken; The lord of that servant shall come in a day when he looketh not for him, and in an hour that he is not aware of, And shall cut him asunder, and appoint him his portion with the hypocrites: there shall be weeping and gnashing of teeth.

There are people who will be ready. Again, there were overcomers in every one of the seven churches who received eternal life, whose names were written in the book of life. Satan had infiltrated six of those churches, and to those He said: *"To him that overcometh those issues. . ."* The overcomer was found ready.

The church at Philadelphia is the one church that Jesus said would miss the time of testing. This church was faithful. This church was trustworthy. This church was true. This church was a Word church, not only hearing, but also doing the Word. This church was faithful unto death. Clearly this is the standard.

If you have to tell somebody to be ready, then it is possible for that person to not be ready, and there are consequences to that. In Matthew chapter 25, Jesus tells a parable that emphasizes the importance of being ready:

Matthew 25:1-13

Then shall the kingdom of heaven be likened unto ten virgins, which took their lamps, and went forth to meet the bridegroom. And five of them were wise, and five were foolish. They that were foolish took their lamps, and took no oil with them: But the wise took oil in their vessels with their lamps. While the bridegroom tarried, they all slumbered and slept.

And at midnight there was a cry made, Behold, the bridegroom cometh; go ye out to meet him. Then all those virgins arose, and trimmed their lamps. And the foolish said unto the wise, Give us of your oil; for our lamps are gone out.

But the wise answered, saying, Not so; lest there be not enough for us and you: but go ye rather to them that sell, and buy for yourselves. And while they went to buy, the bridegroom came;

and they that were ready went in with
him to the marriage: and the door was
shut. Afterward came also the other
virgins, saying, Lord, Lord, open to us. But
he answered and said, Verily I say unto
you, I know you not. Watch therefore,
for ye know neither the day nor the hour
wherein the Son of man cometh.

The point of this parable is found in verse 13:
watch therefore. In other words, be ready because you
don't know the time when the Son of Man will come. *Being ready means to be faithful. It means to be true.*

To be ready, you can't lose your first love. You can't
be a compromiser. You can't deny Jesus. You can't allow
false doctrine. You can't get caught up in all the pleasures of this world. You have to overcome those problems, act on the Word and keep a proper focus. Jesus
gives another parable in Matthew chapter 25.

Matthew 25:14-15
For the kingdom of heaven is as a man
travelling into a far country, who called
his own servants, and delivered unto
them his goods.

And unto one he gave five talents, to
another two, and to another one; to every man according to his several ability;
and straightway took his journey.

The man with five talents makes five more. The man with two talents makes two more. It is interesting what He says about that in verse 20: *"And so he that had received five talents came and brought other five talents, saying, Lord, thou deliveredst unto me five talents: behold, I have gained beside them five talents more. His lord said unto him, Well done, thou good and faithful servant: thou hast been faithful over a few things, I will make thee ruler over many things: enter thou into the joy of thy lord" (Matthew 25:20-21).* He says the same thing to the man that delivered two. Then we get down to verse 24.

> **Matthew 25:24-26**
> Then he which had received the one talent came and said, Lord, I knew thee that thou art an hard man, reaping where thou hast not sown, and gathering where thou hast not strawed: And I was afraid, and went and hid thy talent in the earth: lo, there thou hast that is thine. His lord answered and said unto him, Thou wicked and slothful servant, thou knewest that I reap where I sowed not, and gather where I have not strawed.

He called him wicked and lazy. This servant didn't steal what the Lord gave him; he just didn't produce with it.

Matthew 25:27
Thou oughtest therefore to have put my
money to the exchangers, and then at
my coming I should have received mine
own with usury.

He said, *"If you weren't going to use what I gave you,
you should at least have helped somebody else so that I
received something from what I gave you."*

Matthew 25:28
Take therefore the talent from him, and
give it unto him which hath ten talents.

The Lord didn't give this talent to the man who had
five. He gave it to the man who had ten, the one who
had the most ability or who had done the most for Him.
*"For unto whomsoever much is given, of him shall be
much required"* (Luke 12:48).

In summary, when Jesus was asked about what
would happen at the end of time, He talked about being
ready and gave examples of some people who were ready
and some who weren't. Those who were ready were the
overcomers in the churches.

**Just because you are saved doesn't mean that
you will be in the rapture of the church.** The cold,
the lukewarm, those who have lost their first love and
are not producing for God, and those who are caught up
with the things of the world don't automatically qualify
for the rapture. They are backslidden. That is a hard

concept for people who have been taught that if they have been saved once they are always saved, and thus can live anyway they want to live.

1 John 1:9
If we confess our sins, he is faithful and just to forgive us our sins, and to cleanse us from all unrighteousness.

In order to receive cleansing, we have to acknowledge the sin. You have to ask for forgiveness. *Repentance is not saying sorry with your mouth; it is changing your ways.* When you do, you are cleansed from all unrighteousness. We are in right-standing with God again. It stands to reason that if you have not acknowledged the sin, you are not in right standing with God. Look at the truth in Mark chapter 13.

Mark 13:32-37
But of that day and that hour knoweth no man, no, not the angels which are in heaven, neither the Son, but the Father. Take ye heed, watch and pray: for ye know not when the time is.

For the Son of Man is as a man taking a far journey, who left his house, and gave authority to his servants, and to every man his work, and commanded the porter to watch. Watch ye therefore:

for ye know not when the master of the
house cometh, at even, or at midnight,
or at the cockcrowing, or in the morning: Lest coming suddenly he find you
sleeping. And what I say unto you I say
unto all, Watch.

These are warnings to be ready, warnings to act
and do.

Occupy Until He Comes

In Luke chapter 21, Jesus says that when you see these
things coming, you should lift your head and look for
His return.

Luke 21:27-28, 36
And then shall they see the Son of Man
coming in a cloud with power and
great glory. And when these things begin to come to pass, then look up, and
lift up your heads; for your redemption
draweth nigh.

Watch ye therefore, and pray always,
that ye may be accounted worthy to
escape all these things that shall come
to pass, and to stand before the Son of
Man.

You are to be watchful and stay in prayer so that you'll be ready to escape the things that will happen. It matters greatly how you live.

Hebrews 9:28
So Christ was once offered to bear the sins of many; and unto them that look for him shall he appear the second time without sin unto salvation.

Notice that Paul says that those who are looking for Him shall see him appear again. In other words, they are living life in expectancy.

Titus 2:11-13
For the grace of God that bringeth salvation hath appeared to all men, Teaching us that, denying ungodliness and worldly lusts, we should live soberly, righteously, and godly, in this present world; Looking for that blessed hope, and the glorious appearing of the great God and our Saviour Jesus Christ.

When you are looking for His return, when you live with that blessed hope that He is coming again, then you live every day as if He could come any second. I am using Scripture after Scripture because I know what I was taught. I know what many of you have been taught. My preacher said one thing, but I read what Jesus said in Scripture. I said, *"Who am I going to believe? My preacher or Jesus?"*

Luke 19:13
And he called his ten servants, and de-livered them ten pounds, and said unto them, Occupy till I come.

The word *occupy* means to *stay busy.* This parable is about making God rich. God does not measure His wealth in silver and gold; **God measures His wealth in souls.** The individual that doesn't do what God has called them to do is not pleasing to God. You are not pleasing God if you have not found the place God has called you to be and doing what He has called you to do. Only then are you productive. Only then are you fulfill-ing His plan for you. He called you for a specific time, to a specific place and to some specific people in order to do a specific thing. You do not get rewarded for any-thing outside of that. The rest of it is all wood, hay and stubble.

That's why the first thing I did when God called me to the ministry was take months praying about one thing: *"Lord, what have you called me to do? Where do you want me to be?"* When He told me that, the next thing I did was to act on it so I could be pleasing to God. Faith's purpose is to fulfill that.

Hebrews 11:6
But without faith it is impossible to please

> him: for he that cometh to God must
> believe that he is, and that he is a re-
> warder of them that diligently seek him.

You must diligently seek Him in order to find out what He wants and then to do it. That is what the walk of faith is about. It is not about how much money you can get. It is not about how many houses you can get. It is not about all the other stuff you can get. It is about making God rich. If you are not doing what God called you to do, you are going to be surprised at the rapture when you are still here!

Let's say I started a company called *Keith and Children* and hired my son to sell my product in this region. I come back a year later and ask, *"How many units of my product did you sell?"*

What if he were to say, *"None, but I want a promotion."*

I would say, *"Are you out of your mind? I should fire you."*

What makes you think God became stupid? The next time you want to argue with God and He says, *"I want you to do something"* and you refuse, don't expect a promotion! This is serious stuff. That's why He said that the people who read and do what is in Revelation are blessed. You can't just read the book; you have to change your ways and act on it.

Revelation 3:8

> I know thy works: behold, I have set

> before thee an open door, and no man
> can shut it: for thou hast a little strength,
> and hast kept my word, and hast not
> denied my name.

God is expecting us not only to keep the Word written to us, but also to keep the Word that He has spoken to us. That is why you can't just walk away. You can't say, *"I don't want to do this any more. The people made me mad. I am tired of it."*

Let me tell you. Whatever God sent you to do, He expects you to do that until He tells you otherwise. I don't care what happens. God didn't find out something all of a sudden. God knew the future before you found it out. In fact, He knew it before He talked to you. Get in God's will and stay in it!

Restrain the Man of Sin

In Second Thessalonians, the Apostle Paul has a discussion with the church there about things that had been revealed to him. The Apostle Paul would be in a place up to three years and then move on. He'd write letters to his former churches and come back and visit. At times people would get involved with other teachers who taught things contrary to what Paul had taught, and he would have to correct the errors.

2 Thessalonians 2:1-2

Now we beseech you, brethren, by the
coming of our Lord Jesus Christ, and by

our gathering together unto him, That
ye be not soon shaken in mind, or be
troubled, neither by spirit, nor by word,
nor by letter as from us, as that the day
of Christ is at hand.

False teachers had come, saying that Jesus had
already returned and that the day of Christ was now
happening, that He would set up the literal kingdom on
the Earth, or what we will later call the millennial reign
of Jesus. Paul went on to correct that.

2 Thessalonians 2:3-8

Let no man deceive you by any means:
for that day shall not come, except
there come a falling away first, and that
man of sin be revealed, the son of perdition; Who opposeth and exalteth himself
above all that is called God, or that is
worshipped; so that he as God sitteth in
the temple of God, shewing himself that
he is God.

Remember ye not, that, when I was yet
with you, I told you these things? And
now ye know what withholdeth that he
might be revealed in his time. For the
mystery of iniquity doth already work:
only he who now letteth will let, until he
be taken out of the way. And then shall

that Wicked be revealed, whom the
Lord shall consume with the spirit of his
mouth, and shall destroy with the brightness of his coming.

Something, or someone, is restraining this man of
sin, this man of destruction–the man we will later call
the Antichrist. This man can only be revealed when *"he
that letteth will let,"* or when those who are restraining
him are removed or caught up, when they are out of the
way.

2 Thessalonians 2:9-10
Even him, whose coming is after the
working of Satan with all power and
signs and lying wonders, And with all deceivableness of unrighteousness in them
that perish; because they received not
the love of the truth, that they might be
saved.

**The church is restraining this man of sin, this
Antichrist, from coming forward.** You may think
that the Holy Ghost is the one who restrains the Antichrist, but remember that He will never be completely
removed from the Earth as the true church is. The
church is stopping a complete and total outbreak of law-
lessness. The church is the salt of the earth. The church
is the preservative. The church is in the way of what
Satan wants to do, which is raise up someone for world

domination. Satan wants to possess you and the church so he can have full expression in the Earth. He will try to get individuals into positions where they can have the greatest influence on the greatest amount of people. Resist him. Stay true to God. Occupy until He comes.

Chapter 5 • Revelation 5-7
The Seal and Judgments

I n Revelation chapter four, the scene is set before the throne with angels, beasts and the redeemed. In Revelation chapter five, we see that there's a book with seven seals, and no one is found worthy to open the seals, causing much weeping. These seven seals are seven judgments.

Revelation 5:1-6
And I saw in the right hand of him that sat on the throne a book written within and on the backside, sealed with seven seals. And I saw a strong angel proclaiming with a loud voice, Who is worthy to open the book, and to loose the seals thereof? And no man in heaven,

nor in earth, neither under the earth,
was able to open the book, neither to
look thereon.

And I wept much, because no man was
found worthy to open and to read the
book, neither to look thereon. And one
of the elders saith unto me, Weep not:
behold, the Lion of the tribe of Judah,
the Root of David, hath prevailed to
open the book, and to loose the seven
seals thereof.

And I beheld, and, lo, in the midst of the
throne and of the four beasts, and in the
midst of the elders, stood a Lamb as it
had been slain, having seven horns and
seven eyes, which are the seven Spirits
of God sent forth into all the earth.

Jesus had been seated at the right hand of the
throne of God with a book in His hand *(see Hebrews
1:13)*, but He got off the throne, went through the clouds
to the Earth, and appeared to the true church.

The true church was caught up with Him and taken
back, and now we find them in front of the throne of God
with the elders and with the representation of the Holy
Ghost.

Jesus has returned to the throne and is standing,
having seven horns and seven eyes, which are the seven

Spirits of God sent forth into all the Earth. Jesus is able to open the seals!

Revelation 5:7-11
And he came and took the book out of the right hand of him that sat upon the throne. And when he had taken the book, the four beasts and four and twenty elders fell down before the Lamb, having every one of them harps, and golden vials full of odours, which are the prayers of saints. **[Did you notice that every prayer is captured?]**

And they sung a new song, saying, Thou art worthy to take the book, and to open the seals thereof: for thou wast slain, and hast redeemed us to God by thy blood out of every kindred, and tongue, and people, and nation; And hast made us unto our God kings and priests: and we shall reign on the earth.

And I beheld, and I heard the voice of many angels round about the throne and the beasts and the elders: and the number of them was ten thousand times ten thousand, and thousands of thousands.

What a scene! You have 100 billion angels along with the church of the living God from all time—old and new, all generations, all centuries—in front of the throne of God with a huge rainbow. Jesus is standing in the midst with the book in His hands, about to unleash seven judgments. *Notice that the true church is not going to be there for the judgment.*

Revelation 5:12-14
Saying with a loud voice, Worthy is the Lamb that was slain to receive power, and riches, and wisdom, and strength, and honour, and glory, and blessing.

And every creature which is in heaven, and on the earth, and under the earth, and such as are in the sea, and all that are in them, heard I saying, Blessing, and honour, and glory, and power, be unto him that sitteth upon the throne, and unto the Lamb for ever and ever.

And the four beasts said, Amen. And the four and twenty elders fell down and worshipped him that liveth for ever and ever.

The Rider on the White Horse
What else did John see? *"And I saw when the Lamb opened one of the seals, and I heard, as it were the noise*

of thunder, one of the four beasts saying, Come and see. And I saw, and behold a white horse: and he that sat on him had a bow; and a crown was given unto him: and he went forth conquering, and to conquer" (Revelation 6:1-2).

After the church has been taken up, the man that the Scripture calls the Antichrist can begin his work. The Antichrist is now released. Jesus stands before the throne and opens six of the seven seals from the book that He took from the Father's hand.

I have been studying Revelation for thirty years, and I can remember people teaching that the rider on this white horse is Jesus. He is not Jesus. How do I know? Let's look at some pictures of the Lord Jesus in Scripture.

Colossians 2:14-15
Blotting out the handwriting of ordinances that was against us, which was contrary to us, and took it out of the way, nailing it to his cross; And having spoiled principalities and powers, he made a shew of them openly, triumphing over them in it.

The word *spoiled* means *divested*. Jesus stripped them; He wasn't stripped. In *Matthew chapter 28:18-20*, Jesus said that He had been *"given all authority in heaven and in earth."* Then He says, *"Therefore, you go."* Again, this rider in Revelation chapter six cannot be

Jesus because He has been stripped. We also know he's not Jesus because the Word tells us that Jesus has a crown. Jesus has many crowns and uses a sword, not a bow.

Revelation 19:11-16
And I saw heaven opened, and behold a white horse; and he that sat upon him was called Faithful and True, and in righteousness he doth judge and make war. His eyes were as a flame of fire, and on his head were many crowns; and he had a name written, that no man knew, but he himself.

And he was clothed with a vesture dipped in blood: and his name is called The Word of God. And the armies which were in heaven followed him upon white horses, clothed in fine linen, white and clean.

And out of his mouth goeth a sharp sword, that with it he should smite the nations: and he shall rule them with a rod of iron: and he treadeth the wine-press of the fierceness and wrath of Almighty God. And he hath on his vesture and on his thigh a name written, KING OF KINGS, AND LORD OF LORDS.

The rider on the white horse in Revelation chapter six doesn't have a sword. He doesn't have a crown. He has a bow, but he has no arrows. He doesn't have any armor. This is the man called the Antichrist. The tribulation is seven years long, and during the first three-and-a-half years, this man is not acting as the Antichrist as he does in the second three-and-a-half years.

At the beginning of the seven-year period, right after the church is taken up, this man is going to enter into an agreement with the nation of Israel. He is going to be supported by a European Mediterranean group of ten nations.

Russia and many of the Arab nations are going to come against Israel and they are going to get slaughtered *(read Ezekiel 38)*. The Antichrist is going to now need them to help solidify his position. But at three-and-a-half years he is going to break his treaty with Israel, and he is going to turn on them.

There are two reasons why the church is removed: *first,* so that the Antichrist can be revealed; and *second,* to escape the coming wrath.

1 Thessalonians 5:9
For God hath not appointed us to wrath, but to obtain salvation by our Lord Jesus Christ.

No part of the church should ever end up where the wrath is falling. However, if you want to live like the devil and if you want to follow him, then you can put yourself in that position: *"But God commendeth his love toward us, in that, while we were yet sinners, Christ died for us. Much more then, being now justified by his blood, we shall be saved from wrath through him" (Romans 5:8-9).* God intended that the church not go through this time of wrath that is going to be poured out upon the Earth because of their rejection of God.

Characteristics of the Antichrist

Let's go back to Revelation chapter 6 and find out a bit more about this Antichrist. Remember that the title *Christ* means *the anointed one,* as we see in *Acts 10:38* describing how God anointed Jesus with the Holy Ghost and with power. Christ is not Jesus' last name; Christ describes what He is. John had previously warned believers about this man of sin.

> **1 John 2:18**
> Little children, it is the last time: and as ye have heard that Antichrist shall come, even now are there many Antichrists; whereby we know that it is the last time.

In Scripture, the Antichrist–the anti-anointing, anti-Holy Spirit, anti-Messiah–has six names:

- The little horn *(Daniel 7:8)*
- The king *(Daniel 8:23)*
- Son of perdition *(2 Thessalonians 2:3)*

- The lawless one *(2 Thessalonians 2:8)*
- The man of sin *(2 Thessalonians 2:3)*
- Antichrist *(John 2:18)*

The Antichrist is called *little horn* because he rises among a group of ten horns, which are the nations in the book of Daniel and Revelation. They are in what today is called the European Community or the Common Market of Europe. The system of European nations that provide the Antichrist his base of operations is called a *beast* in the book of Revelation. There were beasts before it–the empires of Egypt, Syria, Babylon, Persia, Greece and Rome–but this one, of course, is more deadly than any other.

The Antichrist is called a *king* because he is the head of the European economic community. He is called the *man of sin* and *son of perdition* because his plan is totally evil. He is a *lawless one*, which means a *wicked one*. He is the Antichrist, because he will deny that Jesus is the Christ, and when he does that he is also denying the Father.

1 John 4:1-3

Beloved, believe not every spirit, but try the spirits whether they are of God: because many false prophets are gone out into the world. Hereby know ye the Spirit of God: Every spirit that confesseth that Jesus Christ is come in the flesh is of God: And every spirit that confesseth

not that Jesus Christ is come in the flesh
is not of God: and this is that spirit of
Antichrist, whereof ye have heard that it
should come; and even now already is
it in the world.

The Antichrist is going to deny that Jesus came in
the flesh. He is going to deny that Jesus is raised from
the dead. He is going to totally and completely come
against everything about the Lord Jesus Christ and
Christianity. This man is Satan's human instrument as
Satan tries to fulfill his plan of world domination.

Satan has been trying to control and dominate the
world for generations. He used Mussolini, and he used
Hitler to try and do it, among others. Why? Because
Satan can have expression in the Earth and full power
only if he is able to possess a man and uses this man to
do his bidding. The Antichrist is going to be absolutely,
totally, unequivocally demon-possessed. Mussolini
failed, Hitler failed and the Antichrist is going to fail,
too.

The Antichrist will work out a treaty with Israel for
seven years, and in the middle of that he is going to turn
on them. Let's find out some more about this man called
Antichrist in Daniel chapter 11.

Daniel 11:36-37
And the king shall do according to his
will; and he shall exalt himself, and magnify himself above every god, and shall

speak marvellous things against the God
of gods, and shall prosper till the indignation be accomplished: for that that is
determined shall be done. Neither shall
he regard the God of his fathers, nor the
desire of women, nor regard any god:
for he shall magnify himself above all.

This man has a religious background, because the
Word tells us that he will not regard the God of his
fathers. The Word says that he will not have any desire
for women; in other words, the Antichrist will be a ho-
mosexual. He will appear to be a world-renowned diplo-
mat of the European community. He will gain control of
their armies. He will enter into a treaty with Israel and
break that treaty. He is Satan's tool on the Earth, and
Satan's last-ditch attempt to see if he can win the world
and defeat God.

The Outpoured Destruction

Let's see what else Revelation chapter six says about
this Antichrist, this man on a white horse: *"And when
he had opened the second seal, I heard the second beast
say, Come and see. And there went out another horse
that was red: and power was given to him that sat thereon to take peace from the earth, and that they should
kill one another: and there was given unto him a great
sword" (Revelation 6:3-4).*

The red horse means the Antichrist is a man of war.
War is going to take place throughout all seven years

of the tribulation. At first, he is going to be known as a man of peace, but he will soon be doing everything he can to conquer the world. When people stop being deceived, they will see that he is a man of war. This man is going to have three of his original ten nations turn against him, and he is going to turn on them and defeat them. Look at certain things that come with being a man of war.

> **Revelation 6:5-6**
> And when he had opened the third seal, I heard the third beast say, Come and see. And I beheld, and lo a black horse; and he that sat on him had a pair of balances in his hand. And I heard a voice in the midst of the four beasts say, A measure of wheat for a penny, and three measures of barley for a penny; and see thou hurt not the oil and the wine.

The black horse represents famine, a big shortage of food. When there is war for seven years, there obviously will be upheavals of nature. This time period is going to be marked by a great time of famine, but not every nation will be in famine. Israel and other nations are going to have food.

It is a myth that the Antichrist is going to take over the whole world; he will never take over the whole world.

Revelation 6:7-8
And when he had opened the fourth seal, I heard the voice of the fourth beast say, Come and see.

And I looked, and behold a pale horse: and his name that sat on him was Death, and Hell followed with him. And power was given unto them over the fourth part of the earth, to kill with sword, and with hunger, and with death, and with the beasts of the earth.

He will have European Mediterranean and a few Middle Eastern and North African nations under his control.

"And when he had opened the fifth seal, I saw under the altar the souls of them that were slain for the word of God, and for the testimony which they held: And they cried with a loud voice, saying, How long, O Lord, holy and true, dost thou not judge and avenge our blood on them that dwell on the earth? And white robes were given unto every one of them; and it was said unto them, that they should rest yet for a little season, until their fellowservants also and their brethren, that should be killed as they were, should be fulfilled" (Revelation 6:9-11).

The fifth seal are martyrs of the tribulation. These are not part of the church age; the church age has already passed. Many people will get saved in the tribulation. Many backslidden Christians are going to return to Christ when every person in their family who was saved and doing the will of God are all gone at the same time.

Now, martyrdom is not the only way a person can get saved during the tribulation. People can be saved without martyrdom during the first half of the tribulation. The saved in the second half, however, will be martyrs after the false prophet introduces the mark of the beast. They will have to wait for their revenge until the end of the tribulation period at Armageddon.

The Final Day

Let's take a look as Jesus continues to open these seals. *"And I beheld when he had opened the sixth seal, and, lo, there was a great earthquake; and the sun became black as sackcloth of hair, and the moon became as blood; And the stars of heaven fell unto the earth, even as a fig tree casteth her untimely figs, when she is shaken of a mighty wind. And the heaven departed as a scroll when it is rolled together; and every mountain and island were moved out of their places" (Revelation 6:12-14).* This earthquake is so great that every mountain and every island in the world is shaken out of its foundation.

I was at the top of a hotel in Pakistan once when an earthquake that measured 7.7 on the Richter scale hit. It sounded like a freight train coming, and then the hotel began to shake and things were flying around. My first thought was that I was going to die, but the Holy Ghost rose up in me and I said, *"I am not dying in an earthquake in Pakistan."* That was the most violent thing I had ever been in. I can't imagine an earthquake that rolls up the entire world. I'm sure I don't want to be here for that.

Revelation 6:15-17
And the kings of the earth, and the great men, and the rich men, and the chief captains, and the mighty men, and every bondman, and every free man, hid themselves in the dens and in the rocks of the mountains;

And said to the mountains and rocks, Fall on us, and hide us from the face of him that sitteth on the throne, and from the wrath of the Lamb: For the great day of his wrath is come; and who shall be able to stand?

This is the final day of the tribulation period. This is the day when the heavens will roll up as a scroll. People are going to see God Himself on the throne. The look on His face is not going to be pleasant. Let's read what the Lord says about that in book of Matthew.

Matthew 24:29-31
Immediately after the tribulation of those days shall the sun be darkened, and the moon shall not give her light, and the stars shall fall from heaven,

and the powers of the heavens shall be shaken: And then shall appear the sign of the Son of man in heaven: and then shall all the tribes of the earth mourn, and they shall see the Son of man coming in the clouds of heaven with power and great glory.

And he shall send his angels with a great sound of a trumpet, and they shall gather together his elect from the four winds, from one end of heaven to the other.

He then tells you what your position should be in *Matthew 24:44: "Therefore be ye also ready: for in such an hour as ye think not the Son of man cometh."*

Be ready. Be faithful. After that last day in Armageddon, Jesus is going to set up a theocratic government. All the governments of the world will be under one leader—Jesus. Scripture says He shall reign for 1,000 years; this will be a millennial reign of Christ. The saints of the true church will reign with Him.

At no time will God not have representation on the Earth. When the true church is taken out of the way and the man of sin is revealed, God will still have representation on the Earth. The Word is still going to be ministered. The Holy Spirit is still going to be working. God is going to bring together some folks that are going to continue that ministry. Let's find out who they are.

The Rapture of the 144,000

"And after these things I saw four angels standing on the four corners of the earth, holding the four winds of the earth, that the wind should not blow on the earth, nor on the sea, nor on any tree. And I saw another angel ascending from the east, having the seal of the living God: and he cried with a loud voice to the four angels, to whom it was given to hurt the earth and the sea, Saying, Hurt not the earth, neither the sea, nor the trees, till we have sealed the servants of our God in their foreheads. And I heard the number of them which were sealed: and there were sealed an hundred and forty and four thousand of all the tribes of the children of Israel.

"Of the tribe of Juda were sealed twelve thousand. Of the tribe of Reuben were sealed twelve thousand. Of the tribe of Gad were sealed twelve thousand. Of the tribe of Aser were sealed twelve thousand. Of the tribe of Nephthalim were sealed twelve thousand. Of the tribe of Manasses were sealed twelve thousand. Of the tribe of Simeon were sealed twelve thousand. Of the tribe of Levi were sealed twelve thousand. Of the tribe of Issachar were sealed twelve thousand. Of the tribe of Zabulon were sealed twelve thousand. Of the tribe of Joseph were sealed twelve thousand. Of the tribe of Benjamin were sealed twelve thousand" (Revelation 7:1-8).

These are 144,000 male, Jewish, virgin preachers. Initially, these 144,000 were involved in defending Israel against the attack of the Russians and their Arab friends. They were involved in the great victory that took place. God then calls them to this particular ministry. By the way, Russia and the armies that come against Israel will all be destroyed in one day. Leave Israel alone.

Revelation 7:9-17
After this I beheld, and, lo, a great multitude, which no man could number, of all nations, and kindreds, and people, and tongues, stood before the throne, and before the Lamb, clothed with white robes, and palms in their hands; And cried with a loud voice, saying, Salvation to our God which sitteth upon the throne, and unto the Lamb.

And all the angels stood round about the throne, and about the elders and the four beasts, and fell before the throne on their faces, and worshipped God, Saying, Amen: Blessing, and glory, and wisdom, and thanksgiving, and honour, and power, and might, be unto our God for ever and ever. Amen.

And one of the elders answered, saying unto me, What are these which are arrayed in white robes? and whence came they? And I said unto him, Sir, thou knowest. And he said to me, These are they which came out of great tribu-

lation, and have washed their robes,
and made them white in the blood of
the Lamb. Therefore are they before the
throne of God, and serve him day and
night in his temple: and he that sitteth
on the throne shall dwell among them.

They shall hunger no more, neither thirst
any more; neither shall the sun light on
them, nor any heat. For the Lamb which
is in the midst of the throne shall feed
them, and shall lead them unto living
fountains of waters: and God shall wipe
away all tears from their eyes.

The elder asks, *"Who are these?"* This is a different group than those who were caught up at the end of
the church age and the beginning of the tribulation and
subsequent revelation of the Antichrist. There are *six
things* about this group which identifies these 144,000
men as being different, some of which we see later in
Revelation chapter 14.

One, they will be given immunity. No matter what
Satan tries to do, he can't take them out. *Two*, they will
have a very effective ministry. *Three*, they will have a
four-year ministry. *Four*, these 144,000 will be unmar-
ried. *Five*, they will be redeemed. *Six*, they will be called
the firstfruits.

Two of the twelve tribes of Israel are different
than the original twelve of the Old Testament. Dan

and Ephraim lost their inheritance because they were the two worst idolaters. They were the most rebellious, so God substituted those two tribes with Levi, or the priesthood, and Joseph. Not only that, because of the ministry of the 144,000 Jewish ministers, most of the nation of Israel and many Gentiles are saved through their ministries and are caught up before the throne.

Many people are going to accept the Lord because of their ministries, but these converts are translated and spared from the wrath of the Antichrist at mid-tribulation. Antichrist wants them all dead. The seventh seal is not opened until these Jewish ministers carry out their ministry.

Again, this group of converts is not the true church of Revelation chapters four and five. Let me give you some of the differences between the two groups. The true church company that is caught up at the end of the church age meets Jesus in the air, and the dead are resurrected. They have crowns of gold. They sit on thrones. They sing a new song, and they are kings and priests reigning with the Lord.

This great multitude of converts are not met in the air. The dead are not resurrected. They have no crowns of gold. They have no thrones. They have no new songs. And they are identified as servants. This is an entirely different group. But again, even though the rapture of this group shows you that there is another chance to be caught up, **I strongly urge you to do whatever is necessary to be ready to make the first flight.**

Chapter 6 • Revelation 8-11
The Destruction Beginning at Mid-Tribulation

One of the issues in trying to understand Revelation is that it's not written in chronological order. Sometimes there's a scene in Heaven and a scene on Earth, but these are not occurring within the same time frame. Ten major events begin at mid-tribulation. We have looked at some of these events, and we'll look at others in more detail in this chapter.

- The Antichrist is going to break with Israel.
- The tribulation saints are going to be caught up.
- Earthquakes are going to occur.
- The Antichrist is going to make war with Israel.
- The Antichrist is going to do all he can to destroy any religious system.
- He is going to set up in Jerusalem.

- He is going to have a false prophet who declares
  that people have to take the mark of the beast
  in his effort to control all money, all business
  and all commerce.
- Two witnesses are going to minister.
- Angels are going to minister.
- The plagues are going to be controlled by the
  two witnesses.

The First Four Plagues

In chapter six, the Lamb was opening seven seals, but
we don't see the opening of the seventh seal until chapter eight. This event results in the releasing of plagues
on the Earth.

Revelation 8:1-6

And when he had opened the seventh
seal, there was silence in heaven about
the space of half an hour. And I saw the
seven angels which stood before God;
and to them were given seven trumpets.

And another angel came and stood
at the altar, having a golden censer;
and there was given unto him much
incense, that he should offer it with the
prayers of all saints upon the golden
altar which was before the throne. And
the smoke of the incense, which came
with the prayers of the saints, ascended

up before God out of the angel's hand. And the angel took the censer, and filled it with fire of the altar, and cast it into the earth: and there were voices, and thunderings, and lightnings, and an earthquake. And the seven angels which had the seven trumpets prepared themselves to sound.

You can call these the seven judgments; they are the plagues, and these plagues are controlled by the two witnesses, who are in front of the Antichrist's headquarters every day telling the world he is false. They are telling the world what is going to happen to him and his false prophet. They are telling the world that Jesus is coming. The Antichrist, who is anti-God, hates all religion, and he certainly hates all Christians. He is going to do everything he can to try and kill these witnesses, these two prophets of God, who will call down plagues.

Revelation 8:7-8
The first angel sounded, and there followed hail and fire mingled with blood, and they were cast upon the earth: and the third part of trees was burnt up, and all green grass was burnt up. And the second angel sounded, and as it were a great mountain burning with fire was cast into the sea: and the third part of the sea became blood.

Another issue in understanding Revelation is the awareness that when John is writing this, he is trying to describe what will happen in the future with language and understanding of his time. He has never seen a car, or even a headlight, much less a tank.

The language in this passage is John's attempt to describe a contemporary army on the march, with hundreds of thousands of tanks rolling across the countryside. He doesn't know what he is looking at and uses language the best he can to describe what he is seeing. He sees something like a mountain coming down into the ocean. Today, we would probably call that a meteor, a huge rock streaking through the sky that looks as if it is on fire.

Revelation 8:9
And the third part of the creatures
which were in the sea, and had life,
died; and the third part of the ships
were destroyed.

If a third of all creatures in the seas die–and remember that the surface of the Earth is primarily water–this would cause great distress. And if a third of the ships of all types–military, commercial and pleasure craft–are destroyed, whatever was powerful enough to cause that would no doubt produce a mighty tidal wave.

Revelation 8:10-11
And the third angel sounded, and there

fell a great star from heaven, burning as
it were a lamp, and it fell upon the third
part of the rivers, and upon the fountains of waters; And the name of the star
is called Wormwood: and the third part
of the waters became wormwood; and
many men died of the waters, because
they were made bitter.

A third of the fresh water in the world is now con-
taminated; it is now poisonous, and when people drink it
they die. You are seeing a great deal of destruction.

Revelation 8:12
And the fourth angel sounded, and the
third part of the sun was smitten, and
the third part of the moon, and the third
part of the stars; so as the third part of
them was darkened, and the day shone
not for a third part of it, and the night
likewise.

In summary, a third of all trees and grass are
burnt. A third of all creatures in the sea die; a third of
all ships are destroyed. A third of all rivers and streams
and fountains become poisoned, causing many to die.
A third part of the day becomes dark; a third part of
the night stars are darkened. All of this begins at mid-
tribulation.

Woe, Woe, Woe

"And I beheld, and heard an angel flying through the midst of heaven, saying with a loud voice, Woe, woe, woe, to the inhabiters of the earth by reason of the other voices of the trumpet of the three angels, which are yet to sound" (Revelation 8:13)!

With one-third of the surface of the Earth decimated, another angel declares that there are three woes yet to come upon the world. Again, you don't want to miss the first rapture of the church! You want to live so that you are included and at mid-tribulation are now living before the throne of God, not in a world that is in the throes of death and destruction. Even if you are not in the areas directly affected, you still will feel the effects, because the whole world is interconnected. Let's continue to read in Revelation chapter nine.

Revelation 9:1-3

And the fifth angel sounded, and I saw a star fall from heaven unto the earth: and to him was given the key of the bottomless pit.

And he opened the bottomless pit; and there arose a smoke out of the pit, as the smoke of a great furnace; and the sun and the air were darkened by reason of the smoke of the pit. And there came out of the smoke locusts upon the earth: and unto them was given power,

as the scorpions of the earth have
power.

If you go back and look at the plagues in Egypt
(Exodus 7-12), you'll see some similarities.

Revelation 9:4
And it was commanded them that they
should not hurt the grass of the earth,
neither any green thing, neither any
tree; but only those men which have not
the seal of God in their foreheads.

This plague of locusts is like scorpions. Let's read a
more complete description of them.

Revelation 9:5
And to them it was given that they
should not kill them, but that they should
be tormented five months: and their torment was as the torment of a scorpion,
when he striketh a man.

That great company of those who got saved in that
first three-and-a-half years are now gone, but people
will continue to get saved during this time.

Revelation 9:6-10
And in those days shall men seek death,
and shall not find it; and shall desire to

die, and death shall flee from them. And
the shapes of the locusts were like unto
horses prepared unto battle; and on
their heads were as it were crowns like
gold, and their faces were as the faces
of men.

And they had hair as the hair of women,
and their teeth were as the teeth of
lions. And they had breastplates, as it
were breastplates of iron; and the sound
of their wings was as the sound of chariots of many horses running to battle.
And they had tails like unto scorpions,
and there were stings in their tails: and
their power was to hurt men five months.

These are demon-controlled locusts released to hurt
only those men without the seal of God on their forehead. These plagues are not released over the entire
earth, only in any area that is controlled by the Antichrist.

Revelation 9:11-16
And they had a king over them, which
is the angel of the bottomless pit, whose
name in the Hebrew tongue is Abad-
don, but in the Greek tongue hath his
name Apollyon **[meaning destroyer]**.

One woe is past; and, behold, there come two woes more hereafter. And the sixth angel sounded, and I heard a voice from the four horns of the golden altar which is before God, Saying to the sixth angel which had the trumpet, Loose the four angels which are bound in the great river Euphrates.

And the four angels were loosed, which were prepared for an hour, and a day, and a month, and a year, for to slay the third part of men. And the number of the army of the horsemen were two hundred thousand thousand: and I heard the number of them.

These four Satanic angels were exiled to Earth when Satan was cast out of Heaven. These are the ones that are loose. Look at Jude 1:6: *"And the angels which kept not their first estate, but left their own habitation, he hath reserved in everlasting chains under darkness unto the judgment of the great day."* They have one year, one month, one day and one hour to operate.

Revelation 9:17-19
And thus I saw the horses in the vision, and them that sat on them, having breastplates of fire, and of jacinth, and brimstone: and the heads of the horses

were as the heads of lions; and out of
their mouths issued fire and smoke and
brimstone.

By these three was the third part of men
killed, by the fire, and by the smoke, and
by the brimstone, which issued out of
their mouths. For their power is in their
mouth, and in their tails: for their tails
were like unto serpents, and had heads,
and with them they do hurt.

A 200-million-man army with armored vehicles is
going to arise from the Orient, mainly China.

Revelation 16:12
And the sixth angel poured out his vial
upon the great river Euphrates; and the
water thereof was dried up, that the
way of the kings of the east might be
prepared.

China and China's allies such as North Korea and
others are going to see the Antichrist and what he does,
and they are going to challenge him. They are going to
march eastward from the Orient all the way to Israel to
do battle with him.

Once again, John is describing the colors of fire
coming from a tank; he's describing a flash. He is looking at a battle.

Look at some of the nations this army is going to have to march through to get to Israel: *India, Pakistan, Afghanistan, Kyrgyzstan, Uzbekistan, Turkmenistan, Iran, Iraq, Turkey, Saudi Arabia* and *Syria*.

That Oriental army is going to cut a swath all the way through. China itself could field such an army. China is building offensive weaponry. They are building aircraft carriers and attack submarines. They are getting ready to do battle.

A great war will ensue, accompanied by famine and death. A third of mankind will be killed in these battles. This Oriental army is attempting to get to Israel to fight the Antichrist and his armies. They will be headed east, and the Antichrist is going to decide that he needs to meet them going west to see who is going to dominate the world.

They will wind up joining forces, because there is going to be another army that is going to show up to fight, one led by a Rider on a white horse. This Rider, however, doesn't have a bow; this One has a double-edged sword that comes out of His mouth and an army of saints. We are headed toward Armageddon. The battle is going to take place at the Valley of Megiddo; the fight of all fights is going to be happening there!

Revelation 9:20-21
And the rest of the men which were not killed by these plagues yet repented not of the works of their hands, that they should not worship devils, and idols of

gold, and silver, and brass, and stone,
and of wood: which neither can see,
nor hear, nor walk: Neither repented
they of their murders, nor of their sorcer-
ies, nor of their fornication, nor of their
thefts.

Those remaining on Earth are people who decided
not to have anything to do with Jesus. Now we begin
to understand that the wrath of God was not and is not
prepared for His people. Those who decide to follow Satan and who hate and curse God are going to be recipi-
ents of His wrath. If you want it, you will get it.

Revelation 10:1-11
And I saw another mighty angel come
down from heaven, clothed with a
cloud: and a rainbow was upon his
head, and his face was as it were the
sun, and his feet as pillars of fire: And he
had in his hand a little book open: and
he set his right foot upon the sea, and
his left foot on the earth, And cried with
a loud voice, as when a lion roareth:
and when he had cried, seven thunders
uttered their voices.

And when the seven thunders had uttered their voices, I was about to write:
and I heard a voice from heaven saying

unto me, Seal up those things which the seven thunders uttered, and write them not.

And the angel which I saw stand upon the sea and upon the earth lifted up his hand to heaven, And sware by him that liveth for ever and ever, who created heaven, and the things that therein are, and the earth, and the things that therein are, and the sea, and the things which are therein, that there should be time no longer:

But in the days of the voice of the seventh angel, when he shall begin to sound, the mystery of God should be finished, as he hath declared to his servants the prophets.

And the voice which I heard from heaven spake unto me again, and said, Go and take the little book which is open in the hand of the angel which standeth upon the sea and upon the earth. And I went unto the angel, and said unto him, Give me the little book. And he said unto me, Take it, and eat it up; and it shall make thy belly bitter, but it shall be in thy mouth sweet as honey.

And I took the little book out of the angel's hand, and ate it up; and it was in
my mouth sweet as honey: and as soon
as I had eaten it, my belly was bitter.
And he said unto me, Thou must prophesy again before many peoples, and
nations, and tongues, and kings.

Jeremiah 15:16 talks about how the Word of God is
both sweet and bitter.

Revelation 11:1-2
And there was given me a reed like
unto a rod: and the angel stood, saying,
Rise, and measure the temple of God,
and the altar, and them that worship
therein.

But the court which is without the temple leave out, and measure it not; for it
is given unto the Gentiles: and the holy
city shall they tread under foot forty and
two months.

Forty-two months is three-and-a-half years. The
Holy City will be taken over by the Antichrist.

The Two Witnesses
*"And I will give power unto my two witnesses, and they
shall prophesy a thousand two hundred and threescore*

days, clothed in sackcloth" (Revelation 11:3). This number of days is about three-and-a-half years. The Antichrist is going to take over in Jerusalem, walk into the temple, and set himself up in the temple as God. Immediately God is going to have two prophets of God, two witnesses, who are going to stand up to his face.

Revelation 11:4-8
These are the two olive trees, and the two candlesticks standing before the God of the earth. And if any man will hurt them, fire proceedeth out of their mouth, and devoureth their enemies: and if any man will hurt them, he must in this manner be killed. These have power to shut heaven, that it rain not in the days of their prophecy: and have power over waters to turn them to blood, and to smite the earth with all plagues, as often as they will.

And when they shall have finished their testimony, the beast that ascendeth out of the bottomless pit shall make war against them, and shall overcome them, and kill them. And their dead bodies shall lie in the street of the great city, which spiritually is called Sodom and Egypt, where also our Lord was crucified.

The witnesses can call down plagues any time they wish upon the Antichrist's area of operations, and they do. The great city, Jerusalem, is now called Sodom, because it is the headquarters of the Antichrist.

Revelation 11:9
And they of the people and kindreds and tongues and nations shall see their dead bodies three days and an half, and shall not suffer their dead bodies to be put in graves.

We have television. We have satellite. When the Antichrist attacks Israel and seemingly runs the Israelis out, most of them will be hidden while the war is going on. The whole world is going to be watching. These two men are going to stand in front of the Antichrist's headquarters every day and torment him. The Antichrist is going to try and kill these prophets and finally will accomplish it. Look at what almost the whole world does: *"And they that dwell upon the earth shall rejoice over them, and make merry, and shall send gifts one to another; because these two prophets tormented them that dwelt on the earth" (Revelation 11:10).*

People are going to see those bodies lying in the street. The people will be having a party. They will even send gifts to one another; they will be rejoicing. The dead witnesses prophesied the plague and everything else that had happened, so this will be a number one news story.

Revelation 11:11-14

And after three days and an half the Spirit of life from God entered into them, and they stood upon their feet; and great fear fell upon them which saw them. And they heard a great voice from heaven saying unto them, Come up hither. And they ascended up to heaven in a cloud; and their enemies beheld them.

And the same hour was there a great earthquake, and the tenth part of the city fell, and in the earthquake were slain of men seven thousand: and the remnant were affrighted, and gave glory to the God of heaven. The second woe is past; and, behold, the third woe cometh quickly.

Once again, these two witnesses have been operating for three-and-half years. They are the olive trees. They are the lamp stands. They have prophesied daily of the return of Jesus Christ. Before the end of the tribulation, the Antichrist is finally permitted to kill them, and there is great rejoicing. Their bodies are left to rot in the streets for all to see, but then they are going to be raised from the dead, causing another earthquake, which will be even bigger than the one after the opening of the sixth seal.

Revelation 11:15-18
And the seventh angel sounded; and
there were great voices in heaven, saying, The kingdoms of this world are become the kingdoms of our Lord, and of
his Christ; and he shall reign for ever and
ever. And the four and twenty elders,
which sat before God on their seats, fell
upon their faces, and worshipped God,

Saying, We give thee thanks, O LORD
God Almighty, which art, and wast,
and art to come; because thou hast
taken to thee thy great power, and hast
reigned. And the nations were angry,
and thy wrath is come, and the time of
the dead, that they should be judged,
and that thou shouldest give reward
unto thy servants the prophets, and to
the saints, and them that fear thy name,
small and great; and shouldest destroy
them which destroy the earth.

Earlier in Revelation, we read how saints who had
been murdered during this particular three-and-a-half
year time are under the throne, crying, *"Lord how long
before you avenge us?"*

He says, *"You are going to have to wait for a while
until some of your other brethren are killed."*

Revelation 11:19

And the temple of God was opened in heaven, and there was seen in his temple the ark of his testament: and there were lightnings, and voices, and thunderings, and an earthquake, and great hail.

They are about to be avenged!

Chapter 7 • Revelation 12-13
Deception and the Beast

T he events in chapter 12 move back and forth in time. John records some amazing visions–wonders in Heaven, he calls them–of the nation of Israel and Satan. Central to the story is the reason Christians can live in hope, the reason we can lift up our heads. The woman described in chapter 12 gives birth to a child who is the source of life and hope for every Christian, both those on Earth and those in Heaven. This woman is the nation of Israel.

Revelation 12:1-4
And there appeared a great wonder in heaven; a woman clothed with the sun, and the moon under her feet, and upon her head a crown of twelve stars: And

she being with child cried, travailing in birth, and pained to be delivered.

And there appeared another wonder in heaven; and behold a great red dragon, having seven heads and ten horns, and seven crowns upon his heads. And his tail drew the third part of the stars of heaven, and did cast them to the earth: and the dragon stood before the woman which was ready to be delivered, for to devour her child as soon as it was born.

The great red dragon is Satan himself. Satan and a third of the angels stand up to do battle against God, but they are big losers. They are thrown down to the Earth. You would think that would be enough to cause them to stop, but they keep fighting. Satan still thinks he is going to find a way to beat God.

Satan is there, ready to devour the child that comes through the nation of Israel. That is the Messiah Himself. Jesus is the child that is going to be born of a woman. In an analogous situation found in Matthew chapter two, Herod is trying to find out where the Christ child is going to be born. Failing to do that, he orders every male child two years of age and under to be killed so that he could be sure he destroyed the Messiah. Herod, of course, was inspired by Satan.

Satan can possess human beings! In fact, both God and Satan are aspiring to do the same thing, which is have men and women yield to them, then operate in the earth and do their bidding. Satan is looking to possess human beings, and God is looking to possess human beings. I am possessed by God. Greater is He that is in me, than he that is in the world! One of the reasons God is in me is so He can express Himself in the Earth and get His job done through His power!

Revelation 12:5
And she brought forth a man child, who was to rule all nations with a rod of iron: and her child was caught up unto God, and to his throne.

Again, this man child is Jesus. Revelation chapter 19 says that Jesus is going to rule with a rod of iron, and we've already seen how Jesus was caught up, or raptured, in Acts chapter one.

Revelation 12:6
And the woman fled into the wilderness, where she hath a place prepared of God, that they should feed her there a thousand two hundred and threescore days.

When the Antichrist attacks Israel and prevails, Israel flees into the wilderness to be hidden by other nations. God has a place for them and will protect them, even though the Antichrist will do everything he can to take them out.

The Rebellion of the Devil

In the next verses, we move back in time and learn what happened when Satan rebelled.

Revelation 12:7-9

And there was war in heaven: Michael and his angels fought against the dragon; and the dragon fought and his angels, And prevailed not; neither was their place found any more in heaven. And the great dragon was cast out, that old serpent, called the Devil, and Satan, which deceiveth the whole world: he was cast out into the earth, and his angels were cast out with him.

Because all power in Heaven and Earth has been given to Jesus, the word deceiveth tells you what remains in Satan's hands. Satan does not have power any more; he has to use deception, and he manages to deceive a number of people.

Revelation 12:10-13

And I heard a loud voice saying in heaven, Now is come salvation, and strength, and the kingdom of our God, and the power of his Christ: for the accuser of our brethren is cast down, which accused them before our God day and night. And they overcame **[prevailed]** him by the blood of the Lamb, and by the word of their testimony; and they loved not their lives unto the death.

Therefore rejoice, ye heavens, and ye that dwell in them. Woe to the inhabiters of the earth and of the sea! for the devil is come down unto you, having great wrath, because he knoweth that he hath but a short time. And when the dragon saw that he was cast unto the earth, he persecuted the woman which brought forth the man child.

Have you ever noticed that the entire world–the entire United Nations–focuses on Israel as the oppressor? Satan is behind this. He has tried to kill off the Jews, whether through Hitler or through many men before. Not only does Satan hate Israel, but also he hates their offspring, the Church of the living God. In other words, Satan hates them, and he hates you. He wants them dead, and he wants you dead. He persecutes them, and he persecutes you. He will not ultimately win over them, and he will not win over you!

Revelation 12:14
And to the woman were given two
wings of a great eagle, that she might
fly into the wilderness, into her place,
where she is nourished for a time, and
times, and half a time, from the face of
the serpent.

Once again, the Antichrist will never control the
entire world. Yes, there will be famine and war and all
the other riders on the horses executing judgment. But
there will be places that have food, places that have
nourishment, and places that still will be blessed. Israel
will be nourished.

Revelation 12:15-16
And the serpent cast out of his mouth
water as a flood after the woman, that
he might cause her to be carried away
of the flood. And the earth helped the
woman, and the earth opened her
mouth, and swallowed up the flood
which the dragon cast out of his mouth.

In this verse, the Earth are people who will assist
Israel.

Revelation 12:17
And the dragon was wroth with the
woman, and went to make war with the

remnant of her seed, which keep the commandments of God, and have the testimony of Jesus Christ.

The Antichrist tries to destroy Israel, but they are hidden, and he goes after their remnant–the 144,000 and their converts. Remember, people are getting saved throughout the seven-year time. At the three-and-a-half year point, the Antichrist and the false prophet declare religions to be illegal and say you must worship the Antichrist and his image. If you worship any other, or believe in any other, then you must die in the areas of his control. But before the wrath of the Antichrist can get to the 144,000, they are going to be raptured.

The Beast

The term *beast* is used in the next several chapters of Revelation. When Scripture talks about the beast it is talking about three different things: *the system created by Satan comprised of the governments, the commerce, and the religion by which he has been attempting to control the world; the man who heads the system, or the Antichrist; and the false prophet or the Antichrist's right-hand man.* Another term you will see is harlot, and the *harlot* is the *false religious system* that Satan is promulgating.

Revelation 13:1-2

And I stood upon the sand of the sea, and saw a beast rise up out of the sea,

> having seven heads and ten horns, and upon his horns ten crowns, and upon his heads the name of blasphemy. And the beast which I saw was like unto a leopard, and his feet were as the feet of a bear, and his mouth as the mouth of a lion: and the dragon gave him his power, and his seat, and great authority.

This gives us details of the beast with seven crowned heads and ten horns. This beast is the system created by Satan, with him as its direct source of power and authority. It is a product of Satan's work through people.

The *sea* out of which this beast comes is not a body of water, but *masses of people*. Satan uses human beings just like God. The ten horns are crowns, indicating that they exist as nations ruled by a ruler.

The beast is identified with the dreams, visions, and prophecies in the book of Daniel. In Daniel chapter two, Daniel told King Nebuchadnezzar the dream and vision that the king had, and then Daniel interpreted this dream. The image in his dream had a head of gold, chest and arms of silver, belly and thighs of bronze, legs of iron, and feet and toes of iron and clay.

The gold head was the Babylonian Empire, and the silver breast was the Medo-Persian Empire. The brass of the loins and thighs was the Grecian Empire under Alexander the Great. The legs and the feet and the toes of iron and clay were the Roman Empire.

The Roman Empire, in place when Jesus came, had two major divisions symbolized by the legs and the feet. The ten subdivisions were symbolized by ten toes.

The beast with seven crowned heads and ten horns in Revelation symbolizes the same system as in Nebuchadnezzar's dream. This entire Satanic system of governments, commerce and religion is called the beast.

At the end of *Revelation 13:2*, we see that the dragon gave the beast, or the system, its power. This word power here is *dunamis* in the Greek, meaning *supernatural power*. His seat, or throne, has great *exusia*, or *great authority*.

Revelation 13:3
And I saw one of his heads as it were wounded to death; and his deadly wound was healed: and all the world wondered after the beast.

The beast's fatal wound is the destruction of the Roman Empire. In Nebuchadnezzar's dream, a stone comes and destroys the image. The stone represents the first coming of Jesus. The church age begins with Jesus' coming, wounding that sixth head to death.

The fall of the Roman Empire causes the system to collapse, but the entire world is going to be amazed because the Antichrist is going to resurrect that whole system. The man who eventually heads the system is also called the beast.

The Worship of the Dragon

"And they worshipped the dragon which gave power unto the beast: and they worshipped the beast, saying, Who is like unto the beast? who is able to make war with him? And there was given unto him a mouth speaking great things and blasphemies; and power was given unto him to continue forty and two months" (Revelation 13:4-5).

The worship of the dragon is the worship of Satan. In the last three-and-a-half years, there is much more direct worship of Satan himself. In *Revelation 13:5*, John begins referring to the man who will have authority and run this system the last half of the tribulation. The Antichrist blasphemes many of the people who escape him, the people who are caught up. He blasphemes them because they are in Heaven.

Revelation 13:6

And he opened his mouth in blasphemy
against God, to blaspheme his name,
and his tabernacle, and them that dwell
in heaven.

The raptures that take place are not done in secret. When millions and billions of people disappear, people are going to notice. This man begins to curse the people in Heaven and begins to curse God. He knows the power that is there, and the people who are serving him know this. They know God exists, and they make a choice to hate Him.

Revelation 13:7
And it was given unto him to make war
with the saints, and to overcome them:
and power was given him over all kindreds, and tongues, and nations.

These are not the saints of the true church that
were raptured or the saints of the first half of the tribulation. These are not the converts of the 144,000; they
are already gone. Remember, God will still be bringing
people into His kingdom during the second half of the
tribulation.

The Control of the Antichrist

There is going to be a one-world government. Satan
gave the Antichrist this power and authority; Satan
gave him this assignment.

There is a difference between assignment and ac-
complishment. Just because Satan empowered this man
to attempt to enslave the whole world doesn't mean that
he will be able to do so. Go back to Revelation chapter
six and look at the rider on the white horse, who is the
Antichrist.

Revelation 6:8
And I looked, and behold a pale
horse: and his name that sat on him
was Death, and Hell followed with him.
And power was given unto them over
the fourth part of the earth, to kill with

sword, and with hunger, and with death,
and with the beasts of the earth.

Notice that the Antichrist has power over a fourth
of the Earth; he will never have control over the whole
Earth. There are a lot of people he won't have control
over. For example, he obviously will not control the
Arab nations that are going to have to fight the Oriental
armies marching across from the east to the west. He
only has the assignment that Satan gave him. Who will
he have authority over?

Revelation 13:8
And all that dwell upon the earth shall
worship him, whose names are not written in the book of life of the Lamb slain
from the foundation of the world.

He will have authority over those who make a decision to go with him. Satan has no power except deception and lies, and he can't do anything without a human
to work through.

The Antichrist gets his authority at mid-tribulation
when he breaks his seven-year agreement with Israel
and attempts to make war with her. At that time, God
is going to rapture the converts of the 144,000 and hide
the remnant of the not yet born-again Jews.

After ministering to that remnant and leading them
to salvation, eventually all the remaining Jew's eyes will
open and they will be saved. The 144,000 themselves

will be raptured. This leaves only the converts of the angelic ministry, the angels, and the two witnesses on the earth to face the wrath of the Antichrist, whose area of influence and control is limited to the European Mediterranean area. Verse eight tells us those names were not written in the book.

A Reprobate Mind

How can people who see and hear all of this still choose not to believe in or follow God? Let's look at Second Thessalonians chapter two again.

2 Thessalonians 2:8-10

And then shall that Wicked be revealed, whom the Lord shall consume with the spirit of his mouth, and shall destroy with the brightness of his coming: Even him, whose coming is after the working of Satan with all power and signs and lying wonders, And with all deceivableness of unrighteousness in them that perish; because they received not the love of the truth, that they might be saved.

Can you imagine how much preaching these people have heard since Jesus' death, burial and resurrection—from the church, from the 144,000, from the two witnesses and the angels? After all that, they are still going to decide not to receive the truth, and they will receive the harvest of their choice to worship Satan rather than

God. Paul wrote about these people in *Romans 1:18*: *"For the wrath of God is revealed from heaven against all ungodliness and unrighteousness of men, who hold the truth in unrighteousness."*

The term *hold* the truth means *they suppress it, hold it down, or hide it.* They keep it from getting out.

Romans 1:19-25

Because that which may be known of God is manifest in them; for God hath shewed it unto them. For the invisible things of him from the creation of the world are clearly seen, being understood by the things that are made, even his eternal power and Godhead; so that they are without excuse:

Because that, when they knew God, they glorified him not as God, neither were thankful; but became vain in their imaginations, and their foolish heart was darkened. Professing themselves to be wise, they became fools,

And changed the glory of the uncorruptible God into an image made like to corruptible man, and to birds, and fourfooted beasts, and creeping things. Wherefore God also gave them up to uncleanness through the lusts of their own hearts, to dishonour their own bodies between themselves: Who changed the truth of God into a lie, and worshipped and served the creature more than the Creator, who is blessed for ever. Amen.

Can you see the humanism in these verses?

Romans 1:26-27
For this cause God gave them up unto vile affections: for even their women did change the natural use into that which is against nature:

And likewise also the men, leaving the natural use of the woman, burned in their lust one toward another; men with men working that which is unseemly, and receiving in themselves that recompence of their error which was meet.

That is the result of men having sex with men.

Romans 1:28
And even as they did not like to retain God in their knowledge, God gave them over to a reprobate mind, to do those things which are not convenient.

A reprobate mind is a mind that believes it is doing right when it is doing wrong.

Romans 1:29-32
Being filled with all unrighteousness, fornication, wickedness, covetousness, maliciousness; full of envy, murder, debate, deceit, malignity; whisperers, Backbiters, haters of God, despiteful, proud, boasters, inventors of evil things, disobedient to parents,

Without understanding, covenantbreakers, without natural affection, implacable, unmerciful: Who knowing the judgment of God, that they which commit such things are worthy of death, not only do the same, but have pleasure in them that do them.

Again, this is a description of people who make the choice to serve Satan rather than God.

Still Waiting to Be Avenged
Remember—the martyred saints ask, *"Lord, how long must we wait till we are avenged?"*

Revelation 13:9-10
If any man have an ear, let him hear. He that leadeth into captivity shall go into

captivity: he that killeth with the sword
must be killed with the sword. Here is the
patience and the faith of the saints.

The saints referred to are those who remain after
the rapture of the 144,000. Many, but not all, of these
people will face martyrdom. Why? Because Satan,
through his Antichrist and false prophet, has decreed
that all religion is wrong and dangerous. The only religion that will be acceptable is the worship of the Antichrist and the image that is going to be erected through
him and the false prophet. Other worshipers are to be
hunted down and killed.

Revelation 13:11
And I beheld another beast coming up
out of the earth; and he had two horns
like a lamb, and he spake as a dragon.

This beast is the false prophet, the right-hand man
of the Antichrist. He has a religious identity. He brings
great deception, causing many people on the Earth to
worship the beast's system. This man has occult powers.
Regarding the Antichrist's operations, Paul says that
he uses lying wonders *(2 Thessalonians 2:9)*. The false
prophet has an image created of the beast and threatens
death if people don't worship it.

Again, this is not true for the whole world but for
the areas which the false prophet and the Antichrist
control. Worship of this image introduces idolatry,

violating the first commandment in *Leviticus 26:1, "You shall have no other God in front of me."*

The Beast's Mark: 666

"And he exerciseth all the power of the first beast before him, and causeth the earth and them which dwell therein to worship the first beast, whose deadly wound was healed. And he doeth great wonders, so that he maketh fire come down from heaven on the earth in the sight of men, And deceiveth them that dwell on the earth by the means of those miracles which he had power to do in the sight of the beast; saying to them that dwell on the earth, that they should make an image to the beast, which had the wound by a sword, and did live.

"And he had power to give life unto the image of the beast, that the image of the beast should both speak, and cause that as many as would not worship the image of the beast should be killed. And he causeth all, both small and great, rich and poor, free and bond, to receive a mark in their right hand, or in their foreheads: And that no man might buy or sell, save he that had the mark, or the name of the beast, or the number of his name. Here is wisdom. Let him that hath understanding count the number of the beast: for it is the number of a man; and his number is Six hundred threescore and six" (Revelation 13:12-18).

This beast does great wonders, making a fire come down from heaven on the earth in the sight of men. *The mark of the beast in Scripture is six, the number of a man, meaning incompleteness.* The beast's system is three sixes (666). Therefore, this system is an incomplete operation, which will fail. Satan designed it, of course, and there are three, incomplete failures: Satan, Antichrist, and the false prophet will fail.

Reader, it is important that you have an understanding of 666. Satan can't win, so there's no reason to hook up with him. I am not hooked up with Satan, and I am not hooked up with the Babylonian system. I am hooked up with Jesus the Messiah! His number is seven, and with that number of completeness you get the Father, Son and Holy Ghost, and they win! You have a choice. You can align yourself with Satan, following the world's system, or you can align yourself with God. You can take 666 or 777. I urge you to align yourself with the winning side.

We are living in an anti-God, humanistic, anti-Word of God system that prevails in our educational systems and in our media. We see the rise of every kind of sin. Every perversion we can imagine is no longer shocking. **We are in the last of the last days.** The last days have been since Pentecost. In fact, we are in that sliver of time between Jerusalem no longer being trodden down of the Gentiles and the rapture of the church. Jesus said, *"No man knows the day nor hour,"* but He did say that you will know by the leaves turning on the trees that summer is near. Summer is near and the return of the Lord is near, so we need to be ready!

Revelation 13:18
Here is wisdom. Let him that hath un-

derstanding count the number of the
beast: for it is the number of a man; and
his number is Six hundred threescore
and six.

No doubt you have heard all kinds of interpretations about the significance of the number 666. It is a
computer. It is an implant. It is a tattoo you will have on
your forehead in order to make purchases. You shouldn't
do such and such because it's related to 666 or it means
666–all kinds of interpretations. Forget all that. The
bottom line is that the number six is the number of
man, who was created on the sixth day. The number
means incompleteness. Man, in and of himself, is a fail-
ure without God.

*The number 666 refers to the three individuals who
are called the beast: the Antichrist, the false prophet,
Satan–and the system they run.* The number means that
there are three incomplete failures. Satan tries to take
control, and he fails. His mission is incomplete. He calls
the Antichrist to do the job. His mission fails. The false
prophet is next tasked to fulfill the Antichrist's mission,
and he fails. They all fail. But God the Father, the Son
and the Holy Ghost are victors!

Chapter 8 • Revelation 14-16
Mid-Tribulation to Armageddon and Back Again

U nderstanding Revelation is like watching a movie that shows an event from many different angles and perspectives. Starting with chapter 14, you see events from the point of mid-tribulation. Things happen that run all the way to the last day or what is called the Day of the Lord.

You will then see it from another perspective and start right back at the front of that three-and-a-half years and work your way back from a different viewpoint. If you understand that you are doing that, you will have understanding, because each time you go through you receive more information.

Jesus is meeting the 144,000 at the end of their four-year assignment and escorting them to God's throne.

Revelation 14:1-3
And I looked, and, lo, a Lamb stood on
the mount Sion, and with him an hundred forty and four thousand, having his
Father's name written in their foreheads.

And I heard a voice from heaven, as
the voice of many waters, and as the
voice of a great thunder: and I heard
the voice of harpers harping with their
harps: And they sung as it were a new
song before the throne, and before the
four beasts, and the elders: and no man
could learn that song but the hundred
and forty and four thousand, which
were redeemed from the earth.

The phrase *"before the throne"* tells you that John
sees Jesus in the heavenly Mount Sion with the 144,000
Israeli evangelists who were sealed at the beginning
of their ministry. In verse two, John hears the voices
of many waters, or people. These voices belong to the
believers that God raptured to Heaven four years previously. Before God's throne you now have all of the
believers of the Old and New Testament–the voices of
all of the saints. No wonder there is the sound of many
waters. In verse three, joining the already redeemed,
the 144,000 are allowed to learn the song.

Revelation 14:4-5
These are they which were not defiled
with women; for they are virgins. These
are they which follow the Lamb whither-
soever he goeth. These were redeemed
from among men, being the firstfruits
unto God and to the Lamb. And in their
mouth was found no guile: for they are
without fault before the throne of God.

Of course, these are the first who choose to accept
Jesus as their Savior at the beginning of the tribulation,
and they are sealed by the angels.

Revelation 14:6-7
And I saw another angel fly in the midst
of heaven. And I saw another angel fly
in the midst of heaven, having the everlasting gospel to preach unto them that
dwell on the earth, and to every nation,
and kindred, and tongue, and people,
Saying with a loud voice, Fear God,
and give glory to him; for the hour of his
judgment is come: and worship him that
made heaven, and earth, and the sea,
and the fountains of waters.

When the true church is caught up, God replaces
them with the 144,000 who witness. At mid-tribulation,
two witnesses and angels will be ministering. In other

words, God will always have a witness in the Earth. The story of God, the Word of God and the will of God will always be told. At no point will any man or any woman be able to say that the Gospel was not preached to them.

These angels in Revelation chapter 14 are dispatched to replace the 144,000 and continue the earthly ministry. All nations hear this first angel preach the gospel.

Revelation 14:8
And there followed another angel, saying, Babylon is fallen, is fallen, that great city, because she made all nations drink of the wine of the wrath of her fornication.

This angel rejoices because Babylon, which is the false church, also called the harlot, has been destroyed. The Antichrist is going to use religion to enhance himself in the first three-and-a-half years, but then he is going to turn on all religions except the religion of himself and will attempt to crush any and all religious belief.

Revelation 14:9-11
And the third angel followed them, saying with a loud voice, If any man worship the beast and his image, and receive his mark in his forehead, or in his hand, The same shall drink of the wine of the wrath of God, which is poured

out without mixture into the cup of his indignation; and he shall be tormented with fire and brimstone in the presence of the holy angels, and in the presence of the Lamb:

And the smoke of their torment ascendeth up for ever and ever: and they have no rest day nor night, Who worship the beast and his image, and whosoever receiveth the mark of his name.

This third angel warns mankind again about following the Antichrist, and then he preaches the consequences of worshiping the image and receiving the mark of the beast. The person who receives the mark seals his or her fate, because that person has totally rejected the true and the living God, and will suffer eternal judgment.

The Patience and Faith of the Saints

"Here is the patience of the saints: here are they that keep the commandments of God, and the faith of Jesus" (Revelation 14:12).

If you look only at what you can see, you may think that the wicked are winning. Don't forget the patience and the faith of the saints. Regardless of what you think you see, the prayers of the saints are going up before the throne of God and are kept and will be answered at the appropriate time with the wrath of God upon the unbeliever. Don't you ever forget it! Prayer is hard work. It wasn't intended to be exciting. In 1 Timothy 2: 1-4, we read, *"I exhort therefore, that, first of all, supplications, prayers, intercessions, and giving of thanks, be made for all men; For kings, and for all that are in authority; that we may lead a quiet and peaceable life in all godliness and honesty. For this is good and acceptable in the sight of God our Saviour; Who will have all men to be saved, and to come unto the knowledge of the truth."*

At the churches I pastor, we pray for the prayer requests that people send us. Then we pray for the lost. We pray for those in authority by name. We pray for our president. We pray for university presidents. We pray for military leadership. Why? Because the Bible told us to do it.

Revelation 8:4 says that God collects our prayers, and they are as sweet incense before Him. Some of those prayers will be answered in God's time, but He hasn't thrown away any of them.

God answers prayer, and God moves in the Earth because people ask Him. He needs somebody that is willing to pray enough, pray often and endure in prayer so that He can complete His assignment. Let's look at the patience of the saints.

Revelation 14:13
And I heard a voice from heaven saying unto me, Write, Blessed are the dead which die in the Lord from henceforth: Yea, saith the Spirit, that they may rest

from their labours; and their works do
follow them.

During the last half of the tribulation, saints will
be martyred because they refuse to take the mark of the
beast.

The Battle of Armageddon

*"And I looked, and behold a white cloud, and upon the
cloud one sat like unto the Son of man, having on his
head a golden crown, and in his hand a sharp sickle.
And another angel came out of the temple, crying with
a loud voice to him that sat on the cloud, Thrust in thy
sickle, and reap: for the time is come for thee to reap; for
the harvest of the earth is ripe. And he that sat on the
cloud thrust in his sickle on the earth; and the earth was
reaped" (Revelation 14:14-16).* Jesus reaps the Earth at
His second coming.

Revelation 14:17-19
And another angel came out of the
temple which is in heaven, he also having a sharp sickle.

And another angel came out from the
altar, which had power over fire; and
cried with a loud cry to him that had the
sharp sickle, saying, Thrust in thy sharp
sickle, and gather the clusters of the
vine of the earth; for her grapes are fully

ripe. And the angel thrust in his sickle
into the earth, and gathered the vine
of the earth, and cast it into the great
winepress of the wrath of God.

The sixth angel, who has power over fire, comes
from the altar. He tells the fifth angel to thrust his
sickle into the Earth. He is to gather the clusters of the
vine, the isolated multitudes of people, or heathen, who
have accepted the mark of the beast and have yielded to
its government.

The angel gathers the vine and casts it into the
great winepress of God's wrath, the same one you will
find in Revelation 19:15.

Revelation 19:13-15
And he was clothed with a vesture
dipped in blood: and his name is called
The Word of God. And the armies which
were in heaven followed him upon
white horses, clothed in fine linen, white
and clean.

And out of his mouth goeth a sharp
sword, that with it he should smite the
nations: and he shall rule them with a
rod of iron: and he treadeth the winepress of the fierceness and wrath of
Almighty God.

This angel is going to smite the nations; he is going to slay them.

Revelation 14:20
And the winepress was trodden without the city, and blood came out of the winepress, even unto the horse bridles, by the space of a thousand and six hundred furlongs.

This is the battle of Armageddon, which is fought outside of Jerusalem. This battle happens on the last day of the tribulation. So many men are killed that the blood runs as deep as a horse's bridle over a space of 200 miles. Once again, this is a battle of the Antichrist and his ten confederate nations who have control of Israel and Jerusalem and come out to fight against God. From the East, it is going to be China and its allies and a 200-million-man army. Both armies will come to the realization that they are going to have to join together to fight Jesus, who is coming on a cloud with the army of the saints. Let's look for clues to what happens from Zechariah's prophecy.

Zechariah 14:1-5
Behold, the day of the LORD cometh, and thy spoil shall be divided in the midst of thee. For I will gather all nations against Jerusalem to battle; And his feet shall stand in that day upon the mount

of Olives, which is before Jerusalem on the east, and the mount of Olives shall cleave in the midst thereof toward the east and toward the west, and there shall be a very great valley; and half of the mountain shall remove toward the north, and half of it toward the south.

And ye shall flee to the valley of the mountains; for the valley of the mountains shall reach unto Azal: yea, ye shall flee, like as ye fled from before the earthquake in the days of Uzziah king of Judah: and the LORD my God shall come, and all the saints with thee.

Look at the sword coming out of Jesus' mouth when He comes with the army of the saints and does battle with approximately 300-400 million men in one area.

Zechariah 14:12a
And this shall be the plague wherewith the LORD will smite all the people that have fought against Jerusalem.

This plague will be the sword out of Jesus' mouth. Remember, the sword is double-edged because it cuts two ways. One side of the sword is a blessing, and the other side of the sword is the curse. If you obey the Word of God you get the blessing, cutting loose all that

Satan is trying to bind you with. But if you come against God, the sword cuts you loose from the blessing and introduces you to the curse.

Zechariah 14:12-18

And this shall be the plague wherewith the LORD will smite all the people that have fought against Jerusalem; Their flesh shall fall away while they stand upon their feet, and their eyes shall melt away in their holes, and their tongue shall melt away in their mouth.

And it shall come to pass in that day, that a great tumult **[confusion]** from the LORD shall be among them; and they shall lay hold every one on the hand of his neighbor, and his hand shall rise up against the hand of his neighbour. And Judah also shall fight at Jerusalem; and the wealth of all the heathen round about shall be gathered together, gold, and silver, and apparel, in great abundance.

And so shall be the plague of the horse, of the mule, of the camel, and of the ass, and of all the beasts that shall be in these tents, as this plague. And it shall come to pass, that every one that is left

of all the nations which came against
Jerusalem shall even go up from year
to year to worship the King, the LORD of
hosts, and to keep the feast of taber-
nacles.

The plague is so bad that it kills millions upon millions standing on their feet. Furthermore, all the tanks,
aircraft, artillery pieces, guns and grenades will turn on
each other. Think about the size of this area—no doubt
200 miles long. Everything in that battle area will be
killed.

That is the winepress of the wrath of God. This is
going to be a tumult where everyone goes mad. Men will
be falling over and dying, their skin falling off and their
eyes melting. I am going to see that fight, because I am
going to be in the army of the saints.

Back to Mid-Tribulation

*"And I saw another sign in heaven, great and marvel-
lous, seven angels having the seven last plagues; for in
them is filled up the wrath of God" (Revelation 15:1).*
We've gone from the midpoint of tribulation to the last
day. Let's head back to the midpoint again.

Revelation 15:2

And I saw as it were a sea of glass mingled with fire: and them that had gotten
the victory over the beast, and over his
image, and over his mark, and over the

number of his name, stand on the sea of glass, having the harps of God.

The seven angels are prepared to minister the seven last plagues. In verse two, John sees countless multitudes of people around God's throne. The great crystal sea is the church who supports the saints, who are victorious over the Antichrist, who have come out of the tribulation. The fire is the Holy Ghost.

Revelation 15:3-8

And they sing the song of Moses the servant of God, and the song of the Lamb, saying, Great and marvellous are thy works, Lord God Almighty; just and true are thy ways, thou King of saints. Who shall not fear thee, O Lord, and glorify thy name? for thou only art holy: for all nations shall come and worship before thee; for thy judgments are made manifest.

And after that I looked, and, behold, the temple of the tabernacle of the testimony in heaven was opened: And the seven angels came out of the temple, having the seven plagues, clothed in pure and white linen, and having their breasts girded with golden girdles. And one of the four beasts gave unto the

> seven angels seven golden vials full of
> the wrath of God, who liveth for ever
> and ever. And the temple was filled with
> smoke from the glory of God, and from
> his power; and no man was able to en-
> ter into the temple, till the seven plagues
> of the seven angels were fulfilled.

The smoke is symbolic of God's glory, preventing all men from entering the temple, until these plagues are fulfilled.

Revelation 16:1
> And I heard a great voice out of the
> temple saying to the seven angels, Go
> your ways, and pour out the vials of the
> wrath of God upon the earth.

Again, we have gone from the last day to the midpoint, and we're going right down to the end again. We are going to see what happens to men and women on the Earth who take the mark of the beast, who worship the beast image, and who reject God.

Revelation 16:2-3
> And the first went, and poured out his
> vial upon the earth; and there fell a noi-
> some and grievous sore **[boil]** upon the
> men which had the mark of the beast,
> and upon them which worshipped his

image. And the second angel poured
out his vial upon the sea; and it became
as the blood of a dead man: and every
living soul died in the sea.

We have seen a third of the sea become blood; now
all of it is as the coagulated blood of a dead man. What
do you think this looks like? What does it smell like? No
wonder every living thing in the sea died.

Revelation 16:4-6
And the third angel poured out his vial
upon the rivers and fountains of waters;
and they became blood. And I heard
the angel of the waters say, Thou art
righteous, O Lord, which art, and wast,
and shalt be, because thou hast judged
thus. For they have shed the blood
of saints and prophets, and thou hast
given them blood to drink; for they are
worthy.

These last seven plagues are designed to aid in the
destruction of the beast's system, the Antichrist and the
false prophet. They fall on the wicked, on those who took
the mark of the beast and worshipped his image. The
rest of the seas turn to blood, giving the wicked blood
to drink. That is just punishment because Scripture
says that many of them have killed the saints: *"And I
heard another out of the altar say, Even so, Lord God*

Almighty, true and righteous are thy judgments. And the fourth angel poured out his vial upon the sun; and power was given unto him to scorch men with fire. And men were scorched with great heat, and blasphemed the name of God, which hath power over these plagues: and they repented not to give him glory" (Revelation 16:7-9).

The sun's rays are intensified greatly. Men suffer heat protestation, severe sunburn, and dehydration. Do men fall on their knees and repent? No.

Revelation 16:10-11

And the fifth angel poured out his vial upon the seat of the beast; and his kingdom was full of darkness; and they gnawed their tongues for pain. And blasphemed the God of heaven because of their pains and their sores, and [once again] repented not of their deeds.

When that fifth trumpet sounds, the plague is released, bringing darkness to the entire kingdom. There is no more natural light over all of the kingdom of the Antichrist, the false prophet and his beast system. Still, people would rather blaspheme God than repent.

Revelation 16:12-14

And the sixth angel poured out his vial upon the great river Euphrates; and the water thereof was dried up, that the way of the kings of the east might be prepared.

And I saw three unclean spirits like frogs come out of the mouth of the dragon, and out of the mouth of the beast, and out of the mouth of the false prophet. For they are the spirits of devils, working miracles, which go forth unto the kings of the earth and of the whole world, to gather them to the battle of that great day of God Almighty.

They are being gathered to the battle of Armageddon. The fact that the river Euphrates is dried up allows the army, or the kings of the East, to cross over land into the Holy Land. As these armies sweep across Asia, they kill one-third of the Earth's population. If the population of the Earth is between seven and eight billion, between one-and-three-quarters to two billion people are killed in war in a three-and-a-half year time-frame. It will be the bloodiest war of all times until Armageddon.

Look at the Lord's warning: *"Behold, I come as a thief. Blessed is he that watcheth, and keepeth his garments, lest he walk naked, and they see his shame" (Revelation 16:15).*

Once again, **God is telling us to be ready for the rapture of the true church. Live every day as though Jesus is coming back that day.** We are living in that sliver of time when He could return. Any day could be the day that the true church is caught up with Him in the clouds and the Antichrist and the seven years of tests, trials and tribulations are released. I want to see this only from a seat in Heaven!

Revelation 16:16-18
And he gathered them together into a place called in the Hebrew tongue Armageddon. And the seventh angel poured out his vial into the air; and there came a great voice out of the temple of heaven, from the throne, saying, It is done. And there were voices, and thunders, and lightnings; and there was a great earthquake, such as was not since men were upon the earth, so mighty an earthquake, and so great.

This earthquake occurs on the last day of the tribulation.

Revelation 16:19-21
And the great city was divided into three parts, and the cities of the nations fell: and great Babylon came in remembrance before God, to give unto her the cup of the wine of the fierceness of his wrath. And every island fled away, and the mountains were not found. And there fell upon men a great hail out of

heaven, every stone about the weight
of a talent: and men blasphemed God
because of the plague of the hail; for
the plague thereof was exceeding
great.

This hail, weighing between 90 and 105 pounds,
and the largest earthquake ever in mankind's history
will flatten every city and sink every island. It will ro-
tate the Earth off its axis. This is the last day, the *Day
of the Lord.* With all that is happening, you would think
people would fall on the ground pleading for mercy.
They know there is a God. They know there are saints.
They know the truth. Instead, they shake their fists at
God and blaspheme His name more and more.

When I think about this, my mind just can't com-
pute it. I can't imagine being on Earth with an angel
preaching to the world, two witnesses testifying to the
things of God, and still not surrendering. The redeemed
will be in that army of white, returning on the victorious
side. Don't dare reject God.

Chapter 9 • Revelation 17-19
The Triumphant Rider

W e are drawing to the end of Revelation, and there are some wonderful things for us who are believers. We are the blessed! Chapter 17 deals with the false church. Remember, the false church in the book of Revelation is also called the harlot, and at times it is call the beast's system.

Revelation 17:1-3
And there came one of the seven angels which had the seven vials, and talked with me, saying unto me, Come hither; I will shew unto thee the judgment of the great whore that sitteth upon many waters: With whom the kings of the earth have committed fornica-

tion, and the inhabitants of the earth
have been made drunk with the wine of
her fornication. So he carried me away
in the spirit into the wilderness: and I saw
a woman sit upon a scarlet coloured
beast, full of names of blasphemy, having seven heads and ten horns.

One of the seven judgments an angel reveals is the
plight of the false church. At mid-tribulation, the Antichrist is going to turn on this false church, this false
religion that had helped him into power.

This false church is full of lying signs and wonders,
including occult practices such as witchcraft. The Earth
is going to be full of iniquity. If people believe the lie,
then that is what they are going to get.

John says that it is the great whore that sits upon
many waters. This harlot troubles all the kings of the
Earth, or many of the leaders and many people who are
involved with her. In verse three, she rises to worldwide
influence on the back of a scarlet-colored beast.

This false church of the tribulation is backed by the
Antichrist at this time, and he's backed by Satan. The
wilderness denotes masses of people all over the world
who are controlled by false religion through all the ages.
Satan has always had a counterfeit religion to try and
move people away from the true and living God.

Revelation 17:4
And the woman was arrayed in purple

and scarlet colour, and decked with
gold and precious stones and pearls,
having a golden cup in her hand full of
abominations and filthiness of her fornication.

Exodus 28:8 describes the colors used in the Temple
of God–blue–and the colors that the priests wore–scarlet
and purple. *Blue* defines *what is heavenly in relation to
Jesus. Scarlet* symbolizes *humanity and blood. Purple,*
of course, is the *mingling of blue and scarlet, which
depicts Jesus as being both from Heaven and the Earth.*
Jesus is a divinely made man. There is a reborn man
seated now at the right hand of the throne of God.

The color blue is absent from the false church, as
is Jesus. The Antichrist refuses to identify with Jesus
and will never certify that Jesus is raised from the dead,
that He is the Lord of Glory. He will never certify that
Jesus is come in the flesh.

Revelation 17:5
And upon her forehead was a name
written, MYSTERY, BABYLON THE GREAT,
THE MOTHER OF HARLOTS AND ABOMI-
NATIONS OF THE EARTH.

The name *mystery* identifies the harlot as being
of a *religious nature, spiritualistic.* The name *Babylon
the Great*, of course, identifies the harlot as among *the
original Roman or Gentile system*, or what we call the

Babylonian Empire. Because of the harlot's vast influence on the world's commercial operations, she controls the world leaders who hate her and wish her dead. This system is over all the planet and has a headquarters.

There has been a move for decades trying to pull all people into one religion, saying, *"Yes, we have differences, but we are all serving the same God, so let's all get along and be unified."* The closer we get to the end, the more you'll see this spirit, and the more people who say, *"Jesus is the only way to Heaven"* will be ridiculed and mocked.

Revelation 17:6
And I saw the woman drunken with the blood of the saints, and with the blood of the martyrs of Jesus: and when I saw her, I wondered with great admiration.

Satan will use false religion as one of the platforms for murder.

The Beast Who Was, And Is Not

"And the angel said unto me, Wherefore didst thou marvel? I will tell thee the mystery of the woman, and of the beast that carrieth her, which hath the seven heads and ten horns. The beast that thou sawest was, and is not; and shall ascend out of the bottomless pit, and go into perdition: and they that dwell on the earth shall wonder, whose names were not written in the book of life from the foundation of the world, when they behold the beast

that was, and is not, and yet is" (Revelation 17:7-8). This beast that was, and is not is Satan himself. He is the one behind the entire false church that has come about through all the centuries.

Revelation 17:9-11
And here is the mind which hath wisdom. The seven heads are seven mountains, on which the woman sitteth. And there are seven kings: five are fallen, and one is, and the other is not yet come; and when he cometh, he must continue a short space. And the beast that was, and is not, even he is the eighth, and is of the seven, and goeth into perdition.

In other words, the harlot has ruled over seven kingdoms throughout history and has restored the entire empire system in the form of the European Union. Produced by the seventh head, this system is going to produce the Antichrist who will eventually be the eighth head. The ten leaders have a powerful connection with world church, and so they continue to rise.

Revelation 17:12-13
And the ten horns which thou sawest are ten kings, which have received no kingdom as yet; but receive power as kings one hour with the beast. These

have one mind, and shall give their
power and strength unto the beast.

    The people of the Earth, particularly those in the area controlled by the Antichrist, will be united behind false religion and filled with delusion. They will be convinced by all these lying signs and wonders.
    Religion will be important again and something that the Antichrist will use. Remember, the Antichrist has a religious background, so he understands even though he doesn't believe. He is willing to use anything to buttress his position.

Revelation 17:14-15
These shall make war with the Lamb,
and the Lamb shall overcome them: for
he is Lord of lords, and King of kings: and
they that are with him are called, and
chosen, and faithful.

And he saith unto me, The waters which
thou sawest, where the whore sitteth,
are peoples, and multitudes, and nations, and tongues.

    There will be a tremendous amount of people who are going to be deluded by false religion to the end of time.

The Great Reversal

"And the ten horns which thou sawest upon the beast, these shall hate the whore, and shall make her desolate and naked, and shall eat her flesh, and burn her with fire" (Revelation 17:16). During the first half of the seven-year tribulation, Satan is going to work through the Antichrist to do this. But at three-and-a-half years, the Antichrist is going to turn on false religion because he has to clear the way so that he can declare himself as God Almighty.

Revelation 17:17-18

For God hath put in their hearts to fulfil his will, and to agree, and give their kingdom unto the beast, until the words of God shall be fulfilled. And the woman which thou sawest is that great city, which reigneth over the kings of the earth.

The capital city is where this council of churches, whether it is the current World Council of Churches or some other, is going to be based. It is going to be the place where all of this springs forth, where the kings of the Earth, or rulers and merchants–people who will profit–will strengthen their position until they are ready to get rid of this woman. They have hated her all along.

Revelation 18:1-2

And after these things I saw another

angel come down from heaven, having
great power; and the earth was light-
ened with his glory. And he cried might-
ily with a strong voice, saying, Babylon
the great is fallen, is fallen, and is become the habitation of devils, and the
hold of every foul spirit, and a cage of
every unclean and hateful bird.

The stench in God's nostrils is false religion.

Revelation 18:3
For all nations have drunk of the wine
of the wrath of her fornication, and
the kings of the earth have committed
fornication with her, and the merchants
of the earth are waxed rich through the
abundance of her delicacies.

In other words, there is going to be a big industry,
and many people are going to make money out of this.

Revelation 18:4
And I heard another voice from heaven,
saying, Come out of her, my people,
that ye be not partakers of her sins, and
that ye receive not of her plagues.

There will be born-again people who are part of this
false religion, who will believe it is the true thing. God

is going to expose it to them to let them know that this is not what they think. He will urge, *"Come out, because if you do not, you will receive the same judgment she is about to get."*

> **Revelation 18:5-6**
> For her sins have reached unto heaven, and God hath remembered her iniquities. Reward her even as she rewarded you, and double unto her double according to her works: in the cup which she hath filled fill to her double.

In other words, the judgment that is going to come to her is going to be double judgment. God hates false religion. Violating the first of the Ten Commandments–to have no other God before Him–is a stench in God's nostrils. Many people have lost their lives through false religion. Hundreds of millions of people have been killed through Islam alone all the way back to the eighth century, simply because they would not bow to it. Judgment is about to fall upon her.

> **Revelation 18:7-9**
> How much she hath glorified herself, and lived deliciously, so much torment and sorrow give her: for she saith in her heart, I sit a queen, and am no widow, and shall see no sorrow. Therefore shall her plagues come in one day, death,

and mourning, and famine; and she shall be utterly burned with fire: for strong is the Lord God who judgeth her. And the kings of the earth, who have committed fornication and lived deliciously with her, shall bewail her, and lament for her, when they shall see the smoke of her burning.

There is going to be some form of military attack upon the capital city. The kings of the earth, the Antichrist, and those leaders with him are going to decide to take her out in one day. She will be destroyed in one hour's time.

Revelation 18:10-11
Standing afar off for the fear of her torment, saying, Alas, alas that great city Babylon, that mighty city! for in one hour is thy judgment come. And the merchants of the earth shall weep and mourn over her; for no man buyeth their merchandise any more.

Merchants are going to be making a lot of money from this witchcraft and sorcery. People will be threatened with death if they are involved with religion other than the worship of the beast and the worship of his image, the Antichrist. They will be told that to avoid death they are going to have to take his mark, but at that point people will back off. They won't be consumers, and the merchants will be upset.

Revelation 18:12-13
The merchandise of gold, and silver, and precious stones, and of pearls, and fine linen, and purple, and silk, and scarlet, and all thyine wood, and all manner vessels of ivory, and all manner vessels of most precious wood, and of brass, and iron, and marble,

And cinnamon, and odours, and ointments, and frankincense, and wine, and oil, and fine flour, and wheat, and beasts, and sheep, and horses, and chariots, and slaves, and souls of men.

The merchants have a lot going on, but it is all a lie of the devil.

Revelation 18:14-19
And the fruits that thy soul lusted after are departed from thee, and all things which were dainty and goodly are departed from thee, and thou shalt find them no more at all.

The merchants of these things, which were made rich by her, shall stand afar

off for the fear of her torment, weeping
and wailing, And saying, Alas, alas that
great city, that was clothed in fine linen,
and purple, and scarlet, and decked
with gold, and precious stones, and
pearls!

For in one hour so great riches is come
to nought. And every shipmaster, and all
the company in ships, and sailors, and
as many as trade by sea, stood afar off,
And cried when they saw the smoke of
her burning, saying, What city is like unto
this great city!

And they cast dust on their heads, and
cried, weeping and wailing, saying,
Alas, alas that great city, wherein were
made rich all that had ships in the sea
by reason of her costliness! for in one
hour is she made desolate.

Notice how swift this is going to be—it will all be
over in one hour.

Revelation 18:20-22
Rejoice over her, thou heaven, and ye
holy apostles and prophets; for God
hath avenged you on her. And a mighty
angel took up a stone like a great mill-

stone, and cast it into the sea, saying,
Thus with violence shall that great city
Babylon be thrown down, and shall be
found no more at all.

And the voice of harpers, and musi-
cians, and of pipers, and trumpeters,
shall be heard no more at all in thee;
and no craftsman, of whatsoever craft
he be, shall be found any more in thee;
and the sound of a millstone shall be
heard no more at all in thee.

There is going to be rejoicing in Heaven when this
capital city is destroyed totally.

Revelation 19:1-2
And after these things I heard a great
voice of much people in heaven, saying, Alleluia; Salvation, and glory, and
honour, and power, unto the Lord our
God.

For true and righteous are his judgments:
for he hath judged the great whore,
which did corrupt the earth with her fornication, and hath avenged the blood
of his servants at her hand.

After the destruction of Babylon, John is going to hear many voices in heaven. Remember, this is going to happen right past mid-tribulation. Three raptures have already occurred at this time: the true church, the mid-tribulation company, and the 144,000 Jewish evangelists. God is upset about false religion!

The Marriage Supper of the Lamb

"And again they said, Alleluia And her smoke rose up for ever and ever. And the four and twenty elders and the four beasts fell down and worshipped God that sat on the throne, saying, Amen; Alleluia.

"And a voice came out of the throne, saying, Praise our God, all ye his servants, and ye that fear him, both small and great. And I heard as it were the voice of a great multitude, and as the voice of many waters, and as the voice of mighty thunderings, saying, Alleluia: for the Lord God omnipotent reigneth" (Revelation 19:3-6).

After the destruction and the judgment of the harlot and after God has avenged His servant's blood at her hand, we are going to come to the *Marriage Supper of the Lamb.*

Revelation 19:7-9

Let us be glad and rejoice, and give honour to him: for the marriage of the Lamb is come, and his wife hath made herself ready. And to her was granted that she should be arrayed in fine linen, clean and white: for the fine linen is the

> righteousness of saints. And he saith
> unto me, Write, Blessed are they which
> are called unto the marriage supper of
> the Lamb. And he saith unto me, These
> are the true sayings of God.

The bride is arrayed in fine linen, the righteousness of the saints. The saints at this point are in Heaven, and they are adorning the bride of Christ. *This is the first hint in the book of Revelation that the bride of Christ is not the church, but the New Jerusalem.*

Some people have the misunderstanding that the church is the bride of Christ. The church is the body of Christ. People get confused between identity and relationships. When the Apostle Paul teaches relationships he uses the example of a relationship between a man and a woman. But he is not teaching that the church is the bride of Christ. Paul teaches that the church is the body of Christ. Let's look at the pronouns referring to the body in Ephesians chapter one.

Ephesians 1:21-23
> Far above all principality, and power,
> and might, and dominion, and every
> name that is named, not only in this
> world, but also in that which is to come:
> And hath put all things under his feet,
> and gave him to be the head over all
> things to the church, Which is his body,
> the fulness of him that filleth all in all.

The church fills Him out. You don't refer to your head as a "he" and call your body "she." The body is going to be the same sex as the head.

Jesus as the Rider on the White Horse

"And I fell at his feet to worship him. And he said unto me, See thou do it not: I am thy fellowservant, and of thy brethren that have the testimony of Jesus: worship God: for the testimony of Jesus is the spirit of prophecy. And I saw heaven opened, and behold a white horse; and he that sat upon him was called Faithful and True, and in righteousness he doth judge and make war.

His eyes were as a flame of fire, and on his head were many crowns; and he had a name written, that no man knew, but he himself. And he was clothed with a vesture dipped in blood: and his name is called The Word of God. And the armies which were in heaven followed him upon white horses, clothed in fine linen, white and clean" (Revelation 19:10-14).

We have a look from Heaven back to the Earth and see Jesus riding a white horse in His return to Earth. He comes to make war. The winepress is the same one as in Revelation chapter 14. Jesus again is going to tread that winepress, destroying the Oriental army and destroying the armies of the Antichrist.

Revelation 19:15

And out of his mouth goeth a sharp sword, that with it he should smite the nations: and he shall rule them with a

rod of iron: and he treadeth the winepress of the fierceness and wrath of
Almighty God.

Remember, this is Armageddon, where the blood
will run for 200 miles as high as the horses' bridles.
These armies will be destroyed in one hour.

Revelation 19:16

And he hath on his vesture and on his
thigh a name written, KING OF KINGS,
AND LORD OF LORDS.

To be King of kings and Lord of lords means that
there are other kings and lords.

Revelation 19:17-19

And I saw an angel standing in the sun;
and he cried with a loud voice, saying
to all the fowls that fly in the midst of
heaven, Come and gather yourselves
together unto the supper of the great
God; That ye may eat the flesh of kings,
and the flesh of captains, and the flesh
of mighty men, and the flesh of horses,
and of them that sit on them, and the
flesh of all men, both free and bond,
both small and great. And I saw the
beast, and the kings of the earth, and
their armies, gathered together to make

war against him that sat on the horse,
and against his army.

With this we see that the great supper, the Marriage Supper of the Lamb, has to do with Armageddon. It has to do with the judgment that will take place there, where more than 300 million are dead in one hour and in one place. The battlefield is going to be cleaned up by more ravens and other birds than you've ever seen in one place.

Revelation 19:20
And the beast was taken, and with him
the false prophet that wrought miracles
before him, with which he deceived
them that had received the mark of the
beast, and them that worshipped his
image. These both were cast alive into a
lake of fire burning with brimstone.

Armageddon commences. Jesus defeats the Oriental army and the Antichrist's army and takes the Antichrist and the false prophet and casts them into the lake of fire.

Revelation 19:21
And the remnant were slain with the
sword of him that sat upon the horse,
which sword proceeded out of his

mouth: and all the fowls were filled with
their flesh.

Something wonderful begins at the end of that
battle: a 1000-year reign of Jesus on the Earth. Jesus'
feet land on Mt. Moriah. All of the armies of the Earth
are defeated. Jesus sets up a kingdom in Jerusalem, and
the saints will reign on the earth with Him for one thousand years. There will be people alive on Earth who will
have survived all of this. There will be people who will
be born during this thousand-year reign. This will be an
amazing time of peace!

Chapter 10 • Revelation 20-22
The New Heaven and New Earth

We are at the last two chapters of the book of Revelation. We have heard God's instruction to the seven churches, witnessed the raptured church around the throne of God ushering in the Tribulation, and seen God's witnesses throughout the tribulation period: the 144,000 Jewish evangelists, the two prophets and the angels. We have seen the destruction that Satan has released on the Earth through the Antichrist, the beast and the harlot.

Jesus has triumphed, however, defeating the armies of the Earth in their last stand at Armageddon and ushering in the millennial reign of peace. Let's look at the next vision of John.

Revelation 20:1-3
And I saw an angel come down from heaven, having the key of the bottomless pit and a great chain in his hand, And he laid hold on the dragon, that old serpent, which is the Devil, and Satan, and bound him a thousand years,

And cast him into the bottomless pit, and shut him up, and set a seal upon him, that he should deceive the nations no more, till the thousand years should be fulfilled: and after that he must be loosed a little season.

Not only is the false prophet and the Antichrist put into the lake of fire, but also Satan is bound and thrown into a sealed pit. For a thousand years, people will be born who are not susceptible Satan's deceit and trickery. People are going to live as long as they did in Genesis.

Scripture says that if a person dies at 100 years of age during this time, he will be considered to have been an infant that died. Satan has a connection to most, but not all, sickness and disease in the Earth, and without him operating in the Earth, few people will be dying of sickness and disease.

Without his deceit, during this thousand-year reign of Christ the lion will lie down with the lamb. There will be one thousand years of peace, and the government will be run by the saints.

Isaiah 9:6

For unto us a child is born, unto us a son is given: and the government shall be upon his shoulder: and his name shall be called Wonderful, Counsellor, The mighty God, The everlasting Father, The Prince of Peace.

Peace will be reigning on the Earth. No one will be studying war any more; there will be no need for military schools at West Point and Annapolis.

The saints will reign with Him—one of you may be the next governor of Michigan or Texas. That is going to be a wonderful time!

Revelation 20:4

And I saw thrones, and they sat upon them, and judgment was given unto them: and I saw the souls of them that were beheaded for the witness of Jesus, and for the word of God, and which had not worshipped the beast, neither his image, neither had received his mark upon their foreheads, or in their hands; and they lived and reigned with Christ a thousand years.

Notice that the word *thrones* is plural. If He is King of kings, He will have a throne, but other kings will have thrones, also. The saints of the tribulation will be rewarded, beginning with their rule of the nations the first day of the millennium.

Revelation 20:5

But the rest of the dead lived not again until the thousand years were finished. This is the first resurrection.

The wicked dead, plus those people destroyed at the coming of Jesus and His armies, don't live again until the earthly reign of Jesus ends.

Revelation 20:6-7

Blessed and holy is he that hath part in the first resurrection: on such the second death hath no power, but they shall be priests of God and of Christ, and shall reign with him a thousand years. And when the thousand years are expired, Satan shall be loosed out of his prison.

Satan is loosed because God is just. The people upon the Earth at this time and those who are born during this time will be people who did not have the opportunity to choose that you and I had. There will be people who never had to deal with Satan. They will have an opportunity to choose whom they want to serve; thus, Satan will be loosed out of that pit at the end of the millennial reign for a very short time.

Open to Deception, Again

"And shall go out to deceive the nations which are in the four quarters of the earth, Gog, and Magog, to gather them together to battle: the number of whom is as the sand of the sea" (Revelation 20:8).

In other words, there are going to be a lot of people who are going to follow Satan rather than Jesus, who is on the throne. There is peace, and then Satan comes out in an attempt to deceive people. You would think people would say, *"Things are good! Get out of here, Satan!"* Instead, they will be open to deception.

Revelation 20:9

And they went up on the breadth of the earth, and compassed the camp of the saints about, and the beloved city: and fire came down from God out of heaven, and devoured them.

With Satan as their leader, the people numbering as many as the sand of the sea surround the world capital, Jerusalem, in an attempt to take down God and His plan. They are devoured by fire from Heaven in one moment!

"And the devil that deceived them was cast into the lake of fire and brimstone, where the beast and the false prophet are, and shall be tormented day and night for ever and ever" (Revelation 20:10). Satan's punishment is eternal damnation and fire.

Revelation 20:11-15

And I saw a great white throne, and him that sat on it, from whose face the earth and the heaven fled away; and there was found no place for them. And I saw the dead, small and great, stand before God; and the books were opened: and another book was opened, which is the book of life **[the Bible]**: and the dead were judged out of those things which were written in the books, according to their works.

And the sea gave up the dead which were in it; and death and hell delivered up the dead which were in them: and they were judged every man according to their works. And death and hell were cast into the lake of fire. This is the second death. And whosoever was not found written in the book of life was cast into the lake of fire.

In Heaven, the Great White Throne judgment occurs with God on the throne. This is the last judgment. Earth and Heaven have literally passed away and been burnt up. The unrighteous, or the wicked dead, are judged from God's books, including the Book of Life. Notice that only the dead–the wicked from all ages–stand before the throne. The believers have already received their rewards. All whose names are not in the Book of Life are found guilty and cast into the lake of fire, the state of eternal death.

The New Jerusalem

"And I saw a new heaven and a new earth: for the first heaven and the first earth were passed away; and there was no more sea. And I John saw the holy city, new Jerusalem, coming down from God out of heaven, prepared as a bride adorned for her husband" (Revelation 21:1-2).

John sees a New Heaven and a New Earth at the time of the last judgment. Notice he says that there is no more sea. The New Jerusalem is occupied. It comes down from God. It comes down out of Heaven after the judgment. I am looking forward to dwelling in the New Jerusalem!

Revelation 21:3-8

And I heard a great voice out of heaven saying, Behold, the tabernacle of God is with men, and he will dwell with them, and they shall be his people, and God himself shall be with them, and be their God.

And God shall wipe away all tears from their eyes; and there shall be no more death, neither sorrow, nor crying, neither shall there be any more pain: for the former things are passed away. And he that sat upon the throne said, Behold, I make all things new. And he said unto me, Write: for these words are true and faithful.

And he said unto me, It is done. I am Alpha and Omega, the beginning and the end. I will give unto him that is athirst of the fountain of the water of life freely. He that overcometh shall inherit all things; and I will be his God, and he shall be my son.

But the fearful, and unbelieving, and the abominable, and murderers, and whoremongers, and sorcerers, and idolaters, and all liars, shall have their part in the lake which burneth with fire and brimstone: which is the second death.

Once again, He issues the warning: *"This is what you get if you stick with me and do what I say. And this is what happens if you don't."* He's describing the New Jerusalem in great detail—one more time, He's saying not to be part of the Great White Throne judgment.

Revelation 21:9
And there came unto me one of the seven angels which had the seven vials full of the seven last plagues, and talked

with me, saying, Come hither, I will shew thee the bride, the Lamb's wife.

Who is the bride of Christ?

Revelation 21:10
And he carried me away in the spirit to a great and high mountain, and shewed me that great city, the holy Jerusalem, descending out of heaven from God.

Christ's wife is the New Jerusalem.

Revelation 21:11-14
Having the glory of God: and her light was like unto a stone most precious, even like a jasper stone, clear as crystal; And had a wall great and high, and had twelve gates, and at the gates twelve angels, and names written thereon, which are the names of the twelve tribes of the children of Israel: On the east three gates; on the north three gates; on the south three gates; and on the west three gates. And the wall of the city had twelve foundations, and in them the names of the twelve apostles of the Lamb.

The New Jerusalem has a great wall, which contains twelve gates. Each gate is kept by an angel, and it holds a name of one of Israel's twelve tribes. The wall has twelve foundations, each of which has the name of one of Jesus' twelve disciples. You have representation of both the old and new.

Revelation 21:15-17
And he that talked with me had a golden reed to measure the city, and the gates thereof, and the wall thereof.

And the city lieth foursquare, and the length is as large as the breadth: and he measured the city with the reed, twelve thousand furlongs. The length and the breadth and the height of it are equal. And he measured the wall thereof, an hundred and forty and four cubits, according to the measure of a man, that is, of the angel.

The city lies foursquare; it's length, breadth, and height are equal. The wall measures twenty-two stories high, and the total area of the city's base is 1,500 miles square, which is 2,250,000 square miles. That city spans an area from the Appalachian Mountains on the East Coast to the Rocky Mountains, from the Canadian border to the Gulf of Mexico.

God is the Architect. A man of God, a friend of mine, was caught up into Heaven. The place the Lord showed him was done in the motif and the artwork that he loves. *"Lord is this mine?"* he asked. He said that words couldn't really describe the beauty of it. That sounds like God to me! Your Father knows what you like!

Revelation 21:18-21
And the building of the wall of it was of jasper: and the city was pure gold, like unto clear glass.

And the foundations of the wall of the city were garnished with all manner of precious stones. The first foundation was jasper; the second, sapphire; the third, a chalcedony; the fourth, an emerald; The fifth, sardonyx; the sixth, sardius; the seventh, chrysolyte; the eighth, beryl; the ninth, a topaz; the tenth, a chrysoprasus; the eleventh, a jacinth; the twelfth, an amethyst.

And the twelve gates were twelve pearls: every several gate was of one pearl: and the street of the city was pure gold, as it were transparent glass.

Can you imagine the size of the pearl for each gate? Can you imagine walking on streets of gold?

Revelation 21:22-27

And I saw no temple therein: for the Lord God Almighty and the Lamb are the temple of it. And the city had no need of the sun, neither of the moon, to shine in it: for the glory of God did lighten it, and the Lamb is the light thereof.

And the nations of them which are saved shall walk in the light of it: and the kings of the earth do bring their glory and honour into it. And the gates of it shall not be shut at all by day: for there shall be no night there. And they shall bring the glory and honour of the nations into it. And there shall in no wise enter into it any thing that defileth, neither whatsoever worketh abomination, or maketh a lie: but they which are written in the Lamb's book of life.

There's a New Earth for the New Heaven!

Revelation 22:1-4

And he shewed me a pure river of water of life, clear as crystal, proceeding out of the throne of God and of the Lamb.

In the midst of the street of it, and on
either side of the river, was there the tree
of life, which bare twelve manner of
fruits, and yielded her fruit every month:
and the leaves of the tree were for the
healing of the nations.

And there shall be no more curse: but
the throne of God and of the Lamb
shall be in it; and his servants shall serve
him: And they shall see his face; and his
name shall be in their foreheads.

How did God begin all of this? He created the
Earth. He put a man and woman in it. He told them to
be fruitful, to multiply and to replenish the earth. God
was planning for an entire world populated with people
who were pure, holy, righteous and human, but they
messed it all up. What do you think God is going to do
at the end? The New Earth is going to be populated. The
New Earth is going to have a capital city for the saints.
There will be nations outside the gate of the city. God is
not going to let Satan get one inch of victory. What He
started out with is what He is going to have.

Revelation 22:5
And there shall be no night there; and
they need no candle, neither light of the
sun; for the Lord God giveth them light:
and they shall reign for ever and ever.

179

The inhabitants of the New Earth don't need any electricity. They don't need any power plants. They don't need the light of the sun, for the Lord God gives them light, and they shall reign for ever and ever.

Revelation 22:6-11
And he said unto me, These sayings are faithful and true: and the Lord God of the holy prophets sent his angel to shew unto his servants the things which must shortly be done.

Behold, I come quickly: blessed is he that keepeth the sayings of the prophecy of this book. And I John saw these things, and heard them. And when I had heard and seen, I fell down to worship before the feet of the angel which shewed me these things.

Then saith he unto me, See thou do it not: for I am thy fellowservant, and of thy brethren the prophets, and of them which keep the sayings of this book: worship God. And he saith unto me, Seal not the sayings of the prophecy of this book: for the time is at hand.

He that is unjust, let him be unjust still: and he which is filthy, let him be filthy still: and he that is righteous, let him be righteous still: and he that is holy, let him be holy still.

Make up your mind. There is no middle ground. Either go with God all the way or go with Satan all the way. God can't stand lukewarm.

Revelation 22:12-15

And, behold, I come quickly; and my reward is with me, to give every man according as his work shall be. I am Alpha and Omega, the beginning and the end, the first and the last.

Blessed are they that do his commandments, that they may have right to the tree of life, and may enter in through the gates into the city. For without are dogs, and sorcerers, and whoremongers, and murderers, and idolaters, and whosoever loveth and maketh a lie.

These are those who are now in the lake of fire.

Revelation 22:16-21

I Jesus have sent mine angel to testify unto you these things in the churches. I am the root and the offspring of David, and the bright and morning star. And the Spirit and the bride say, Come. And let him that heareth say, Come. And let him that is athirst come. And whosoever will, let him take the water of life freely.

For I testify unto every man that heareth the words of the prophecy of this book, If any man shall add unto these things, God shall add unto him the plagues that are written in this book: And if any man shall take away from the words of the book of this prophecy, God shall take away his part out of the book of life, and out of the holy city, and from the things which are written in this book.

He which testifieth these things saith, **Surely I come quickly**. Amen. Even so, come, Lord Jesus. The grace of our Lord Jesus Christ be with you all. Amen.

Where are we now? Jesus said that when you see the leaves on the trees, you know summer is nigh. **He said that when Israel becomes a nation again, that generation will not pass away until everything we read is finished.** I am likely to see this before I die. In fact, I am likely not to die. You, too, are likely to be caught up if you are the true church. We are in that sliver of time between the Gentiles no longer controlling Jerusalem and the rapture of the church, the start of the tribulation, and the appearing of the Antichrist. At any point now the rapture of the church could happen.

The Lord is in a hurry. He is gathering as many people as he can. There will be a great revival of much of the church that right now is lukewarm or dead. There is going to be a great awakening, because I read in Revelation that the population in Heaven and in the New Jerusalem is massive. God moves on the Earth because somebody asked Him.

Our prayers are kept before the throne of God and are great incense in His nostrils. He will answer these prayers with a twofold move: with a great revival and great awakening, and with a great delusion and great falling away. All middle ground will disappear, and it will be extremely clear which side you are on. As for me and my house, we choose to serve the Lord. Make that decision with me!

Prayer of Salvation

Heavenly Father, I come to you in the name of Jesus. Your Word says, "*Whosoever shall call on the name of the Lord shall be saved*" and "*If thou shalt confess with thy mouth the Lord Jesus, and shalt believe in thine heart that God hath raised him from the dead, thou shalt be saved*" (*Acts 2:21; Romans 10:9*). You said salvation would be the result of Your Holy Spirit giving me new birth by coming to live in me. I take you at Your Word. Lord Jesus, come into my heart now and be the Lord of my life. I believe that you died for me at Calvary, that you rose from the dead, and are alive forevermore. I receive you as my personal Lord and Savior. Thank you Lord for saving me. I am now born-again.

If you just prayed this prayer, please contact us and let us know. We have a free booklet, *Where Do I Go From Here*, that we would like to send to you. Please call us at 888-909-9673 or visit wordoffaith.cc/revelationfree-gift.

If you would like to pray with us further, please call 800-541-PRAY (7729). We love you and are here for you.

About the Author

Bishop Keith Butler is the Senior Pastor of faith4life churches in Round Rock and Dallas Texas. He is also Founder and Presiding Bishop of *Word of Faith International Christian Center* in Southfield, Michigan. With the support of his lovely wife, Pastor Deborah L. Butler, and their children: Pastor André Butler and his wife, Minister Tiffany Butler, Pastor MiChelle Butler and Minister Kristina Butler, Bishop Butler continues to plant churches worldwide. He ministers extensively in churches, conferences and seminars throughout the United States and abroad with an emphasis on instruction, line-upon-line teaching and no-nonsense, practical application of God's Word.

Word of Faith International Christian Center
20000 W. Nine Mile Road • Southfield, MI 48075-5597
Tel.: 248.353.3476 • VP: 248.809.4306
24-Hour Prayer: 800.541.PRAY (7729)
To order: 888.909.WORD (9673)
wordoffaith.cc

More Books by
Keith A. Butler

Fresh Water Daily Devotional
ISBN: 978-0-9825028-6-0

The Art of Prayer
ISBN: 978-1-931939-27-0

Managing the Family Business
ISBN: 978-1-931939-28-7

God's Not Mad at You!
ISBN: 978-0-9825028-4-6

Living Life on Top: Winning Over Life's Challenges
ISBN: 978-0-9825028-5-3

Understanding the Kingdom of God
ISBN: 978-1-931939-29-4

Entering Into God's Rest for You
ISBN: 978-0-9825692-5-2

What To Do During a Financial Famine
ISBN: 978-1-931939-30-0

When the Righteous Are in Authority
ISBN: 978-0-9825692-0-7

TO ORDER CALL 888.909.WORD (9673)

CALLED TO MINISTRY?

This website is a place for ministry leaders to receive inspiration, revelation, encouragement, fellowship, ministry resources and more through our articles, video blogs, Leaders' Forum and eStore. Our heart's desire is to help you fulfill the vision of your ministry and truly TAKE FAITH to your world!

One of the goals of The Alliance is to establish a network of five-fold ministry gifts who are willing to not only receive from our ministry, but also who are willing to collaborate with other ministry gifts. Through sharing wisdom and successful ministry practices, we can help save the world together. For more information or to join The Alliance, please visit www.woficc.com/alliance.

CALL 248.353.3476 FOR MORE INFORMATION